Preface

Welcome to "Software Engineering Interview Questions & Answers." This book is designed to be your comprehensive guide to preparing for the challenging and dynamic world of software engineering interviews. Whether you're a recent graduate looking to land your first job or an experienced engineer aiming for your dream position, this book will provide you with the knowledge and confidence you need to succeed.

The field of software engineering is ever-evolving, and as the demand for talented engineers continues to grow, so does the complexity of the interviews. Employers are looking for individuals who not only possess strong technical skills but also demonstrate problem-solving abilities, communication prowess, and adaptability. This book is your key to mastering those skills and thriving in interviews with some of the most respected tech companies in the world.

Our goal in creating this book is to provide a structured and comprehensive resource that covers a wide range of software engineering topics and the types of questions you can expect in interviews. We've gathered real interview questions from industry experts and compiled detailed answers and explanations to help you understand the underlying concepts. Whether it's algorithms and data structures, system design, object-oriented programming, or behavioral questions, you'll find it all here.

Key Features of This Book:

Extensive Question Coverage: We've included a broad spectrum of questions commonly asked during software engineering interviews, from the fundamentals to the advanced. You'll have access to questions that span various difficulty levels, ensuring you're well-prepared for any interview scenario.

Thorough Explanations: Our answers aren't just about providing the correct solution; we break down each problem step by step, explaining the rationale behind the answers. This will help you grasp the concepts and develop a deep understanding of the material.

Behavioral Questions: Interviews aren't just about technical knowledge; we've included a section dedicated to behavioral questions to help you prepare for the non-technical aspects of your interviews.

Interview Strategies: Alongside the questions and answers, you'll find valuable tips and strategies for tackling interviews with confidence, from effective time management to communication techniques.

Real-World Insights: Gain insights from industry experts and experienced engineers who share their wisdom on what it takes to succeed in software engineering interviews and the profession as a whole.

Who Can Benefit from This Book: Students and recent graduates preparing for their first software engineering job interviews. Experienced engineers looking to advance their careers by applying for more challenging and lucrative positions. Interviewers and hiring managers seeking guidance in crafting effective interview questions. The path to a successful software engineering career begins with a strong foundation, and this book is your companion on that journey. It's not just about landing a job; it's about thriving in your role and continuously growing as an engineer. We hope you find this book valuable, and we wish you the best of luck in your software engineering interviews and your ongoing career in this exciting and ever-changing field.

AF658032

Table of Contents

Chapter 1: Introduction to Software Engineering

1.1 Definition and Scope of Software Engineering

1.1.1 Question: What is the definition of Software Engineering?
Answer: Software Engineering is a systematic and disciplined approach to designing, developing, testing, and maintaining software systems. It involves applying engineering principles to software development, emphasizing quality, efficiency, and reliability.

1.1.2. Question: Can you explain the scope of Software Engineering?
Answer: The scope of Software Engineering encompasses the entire software development lifecycle, from requirements analysis to system maintenance. It includes designing, coding, testing, and documentation, while also addressing software quality, project management, and process improvement.

1.1.3. Question: Why is Software Engineering important in the modern world?
Answer: Software Engineering is crucial because it enables the development of reliable, scalable, and secure software systems. In a technology-driven world, software engineering ensures that applications are built efficiently, meet user needs, and can adapt to evolving requirements.

1.1.4. Question: What are the fundamental principles of Software Engineering?
Answer: Fundamental principles in Software Engineering include abstraction, modularity, encapsulation, and reusability. These principles help in managing complexity, improving maintainability, and facilitating collaboration in software development.

1.1.5. Question: How does Software Engineering differ from traditional programming?
Answer: Software Engineering is a broader discipline that encompasses not only coding but also the entire software development process. It focuses on systematic, organized, and quality-driven approaches, while traditional programming often involves ad-hoc coding without a structured methodology.

1.2 Importance of Software Engineering

1.2.1 Question: Why is Software Engineering important in the field of technology?
Answer: Software Engineering is vital because it ensures that software is systematically designed, developed, and maintained. It leads to the creation of reliable, efficient, and secure software, which forms the backbone of today's technological advancements.

1.2.2. Question: How does Software Engineering contribute to cost savings for organizations?
Answer: Software Engineering helps organizations optimize their development processes, reducing costly errors and rework. It leads to better project management and resource allocation, ultimately saving both time and money.

1.2.3. Question: What role does Software Engineering play in quality assurance?
Answer: Software Engineering is central to maintaining software quality. It involves rigorous testing, debugging, and continuous improvement, ensuring that software meets or exceeds user expectations and complies with industry standards.

1.2.4. Question: How does Software Engineering enhance innovation and competitiveness?
Answer: By systematically analyzing user needs and requirements, Software Engineering helps companies develop innovative solutions that can give them a competitive edge in the market. It fosters creativity while ensuring stability and reliability.

1.2.5. Question: What are the long-term benefits of applying Software Engineering principles?

Answer: Applying Software Engineering principles results in software that is easier to maintain, adapt, and scale. This long-term benefit reduces the risk of obsolescence and allows organizations to remain agile in a rapidly changing technological landscape.

1.3 Software Engineering Layers

1.3.1 Question: Can you explain the concept of software engineering layers?
Answer: Software Engineering layers represent a hierarchical structure in software development. These layers segregate different aspects of the software, such as the user interface, application logic, and data management, to enable efficient development and maintenance.

1.3.2. Question: What are the typical layers in a software system, and why are they important?
Answer: Common software layers include the presentation layer (UI), business logic layer, and data access layer. They are essential because they promote separation of concerns, making it easier to develop, test, and maintain the software system.

1.3.3. Question: How does the separation of layers benefit software development?
Answer: Separation of layers promotes modularity and reusability. It allows developers to work on individual layers independently, making the software more scalable and maintainable. Changes in one layer have minimal impact on others, reducing risks and development time.

1.3.4. Question: Can you give an example of a software design pattern that leverages layered architecture?
Answer: The Model-View-Controller (MVC) pattern is a classic example. It separates the application into three interconnected layers - model (data), view (presentation/UI), and controller (logic). This separation enhances code organization and maintainability.

1.3.5. Question: What challenges can arise in software engineering layers, and how can they be mitigated?
Answer: Challenges include maintaining consistency between layers, potential performance bottlenecks, and increased complexity. These can be mitigated through effective design, clear interfaces between layers, and performance optimization techniques like caching.

1.4 Paradigms in Software Engineering

1.4.1 Question: What is a software development paradigm, and why is it important in software engineering?
Answer: A software development paradigm is a fundamental approach to software design and development. It's crucial in software engineering because it defines the principles and practices that guide the entire software development process, influencing everything from coding to project management.

1.4.2. Question: Can you explain the Waterfall model as a software development paradigm?
Answer: The Waterfall model is a linear and sequential paradigm where each phase of the software development process (requirements, design, implementation, testing, maintenance) follows the previous one. It's important for projects with well-defined, stable requirements.

1.4.3. Question: How does the Agile paradigm differ from traditional models like Waterfall?
Answer: Agile is an iterative and incremental paradigm that focuses on adaptability and customer collaboration. It emphasizes short development cycles, regular feedback, and responding to changing requirements, in contrast to the linear and rigid nature of the Waterfall model.

1.4.4. Question: In which scenarios is the Object-Oriented paradigm commonly used in software development?
Answer: Object-Oriented programming is widely used when modeling real-world entities and their interactions. It's beneficial for developing complex applications and systems that require modularity, reusability, and maintainability.

1.4.5. Question: How does the DevOps paradigm bridge the gap between development and operations in software engineering?

Answer: DevOps is a paradigm that promotes collaboration and communication between development and IT operations teams. It aims to automate and streamline the software delivery and infrastructure management processes, enhancing efficiency and reducing deployment issues.

1.5 Classification of Software

1.5.1 Question: What are the primary categories used to classify software?

Answer: Software is typically classified into two main categories: System Software and Application Software. System software manages and supports the computer hardware, while application software performs specific tasks for end-users.

1.5.2. Question: Can you explain the difference between System Software and Application Software?

Answer: System Software includes the operating system, device drivers, and utility programs that facilitate computer operation. Application Software, on the other hand, serves user-specific needs, such as word processing, gaming, or data analysis.

1.5.3. Question: Within the realm of Application Software, how is it further classified?

Answer: Application software can be classified into categories like business software (e.g., accounting software), productivity software (e.g., office suites), entertainment software (e.g., video games), and educational software (e.g., learning applications).

1.5.4. Question: What is the distinction between Open Source and Proprietary Software?

Answer: Open-Source software is distributed with a license that allows access to its source code, modification, and redistribution by the community. Proprietary software is owned and controlled by a specific company, and its source code is usually not accessible to users.

1.5.5. Question: How do Embedded Systems and Real-time Software differ in classification?

Answer: Embedded Systems software is designed to control dedicated hardware, often with limited resources. Real-time software, in contrast, is designed to respond to events and inputs within a specific time frame, typically used in applications like avionics and industrial control systems.

1.6 Software Development Life Cycle

1.6.1 Question: What is the Software Development Life Cycle (SDLC), and why is it essential in software development?

Answer: SDLC is a structured process used to design, develop, test, and maintain software systems. It's crucial in software development because it provides a systematic framework for managing the entire software development process, ensuring quality, efficiency, and predictability.

1.6.2. Question: Can you explain the main phases of the SDLC?

Answer: The typical SDLC phases include Requirements Analysis, Planning, Design, Implementation (Coding), Testing, Deployment, and Maintenance. Each phase has distinct goals and activities, contributing to a well-organized development process.

1.6.3. Question: How does the Agile SDLC differ from the Waterfall SDLC?

Answer: The Waterfall model is a linear, sequential process where each phase follows the previous one, while Agile is iterative and flexible, with shorter development cycles. Agile allows for frequent changes and customer feedback, while Waterfall is more rigid and suitable for well-defined projects.

1.6.4. Question: What role does testing play in the SDLC, and why is it critical?

Answer: Testing is a fundamental phase in the SDLC, aimed at identifying and fixing defects in the software. It ensures that the software meets its requirements, functions correctly, and is of high quality.

1.6.5. Question: How does the SDLC contribute to project management and control?

Answer: The SDLC provides project managers with a roadmap for planning, scheduling, and monitoring the development process. It helps in resource allocation, risk management, and ensuring that projects stay on track and within budget.

Online Resources

Chapter 1 YouTube Playlist Link:
Link: https://www.youtube.com/playlist?list=PLzlh_31VWEFoI3TvpCR1YV5zPoqIlSV_e
QR Code:

Online Exam Paper Link:
Link: https://forms.gle/m4hN3aBTnBEvkcD28
QR Code:

MCQ Video Playlist Link:
Link: https://youtu.be/0UA5tEZhrrw
QR Code:

True/False Video Playlist Link:
Link: https://youtu.be/xtzYryZ1mn8
QR Code:

Online MCQ Exam Paper Link:
Link: https://forms.office.com/r/WMkHzWV5uE
QR Code:

Online True/False Exam Paper Link:
Link: https://forms.office.com/r/jfHTV2YAKq
QR Code:

Chapter 2: Requirements Analysis and Specification

2.1 Software Prototyping

2.1.1 Introduction to Software Prototyping

1. **Question: What is Software Prototyping, and how does it fit into the software development process?**
   Answer: Software Prototyping is a development approach where a preliminary version of the software is created to visualize and validate requirements. It allows stakeholders to provide feedback early in the development process, facilitating better understanding and improved final product design.

2. **Question: What are the key objectives of using Software Prototyping in the development process?**
   Answer: The primary objectives of Software Prototyping are to clarify and refine requirements, improve communication between stakeholders, reduce development risks, and ensure that the final software product aligns with user expectations.

3. **Question: Can you explain the difference between Throwaway Prototyping and Evolutionary Prototyping?**
   Answer: Throwaway Prototyping involves creating a disposable prototype used solely for requirement clarification and design validation. In contrast, Evolutionary Prototyping incrementally builds upon the initial prototype, eventually evolving it into the final product.

4. **Question: When is Software Prototyping most beneficial in a project's lifecycle?**
   Answer: Software Prototyping is most beneficial during the early stages of a project when requirements are not well-defined or may change. It's useful for ensuring that the software's functionality aligns with user needs and expectations.

5. **Question: What are some common challenges in Software Prototyping, and how can they be addressed?**
   Answer: Challenges in Software Prototyping can include scope creep, misunderstandings, and increased development time. Addressing these challenges involves setting clear objectives, managing stakeholder expectations, and documenting requirements and changes effectively.

2.1.2 Prototyping Types (Throwaway, Evolutionary)

1. **Question: What is Throwaway Prototyping, and when is it most useful in the software development process?**
   Answer: Throwaway Prototyping involves creating a preliminary version of the software solely for the purpose of clarifying and validating requirements. It's most useful when initial requirements are unclear or subject to change, allowing stakeholders to explore and refine their needs.

2. **Question: How does Evolutionary Prototyping differ from Throwaway Prototyping, and in which scenarios is it typically employed?**
   Answer: Evolutionary Prototyping focuses on building an initial prototype that can evolve over time into the final product. It's employed when stakeholders have a general idea of their requirements, and the goal is to create a base system that can be gradually enhanced with user feedback.

3. **Question: What are the advantages of using Throwaway Prototyping in the software development process?**
   Answer: Throwaway Prototyping allows for quick and inexpensive exploration of requirements, leading to better understanding and reduced development risks. It's an effective tool for managing changing or unclear project specifications.

4. **Question: What are the benefits of Evolutionary Prototyping, and why might it be preferred over Throwaway Prototyping in some cases?**
   Answer: Evolutionary Prototyping promotes continuous user involvement, leading to more accurate final product design. It's preferred when there is a reasonably clear understanding of initial requirements and the desire for a system that can adapt and grow over time.

5. **Question: What are the potential drawbacks or challenges associated with each type of prototyping, and how can they be mitigated?**
   Answer: A challenge with Throwaway Prototyping is that some work may not be reused in the final product. To mitigate this, ensure clear documentation and communication. For Evolutionary Prototyping, potential challenges include scope creep and a longer development timeline, which can be managed through effective project planning and change control processes.

2.2 Software Requirements Specification (SRS)

2.2.1 Software Requirement Specification format

1. **Question: What is the typical structure of a Software Requirement Specification (SRS)?**
   Answer: An SRS typically follows a structured format, including sections such as Introduction, Purpose, Scope, Functional Requirements, Non-Functional Requirements, System Architecture, User Interface, and Appendices.

2. **Question: Why is an Introduction section important in an SRS?**
   Answer: The Introduction provides an overview of the software project, including its purpose, scope, and intended audience. It helps stakeholders quickly understand the context and objectives of the document.

3. **Question: What should be included in the Functional Requirements section of an SRS?**
   Answer: The Functional Requirements section details the specific functions, features, and behaviors the software must exhibit. It includes use cases, scenarios, and user stories to describe how the software should work.

4. **Question: How are Non-Functional Requirements typically presented in an SRS?**
   Answer: Non-Functional Requirements cover aspects like performance, security, scalability, and usability. They are usually presented in a separate section, detailing the quality attributes and constraints the software must adhere to.

5. **Question: What is the purpose of the Appendices section in an SRS, and what kind of content might be found there?**
   Answer: The Appendices section contains supplementary information, such as data dictionaries, sample mockups, or additional technical details. It provides a reference for readers who need more in-depth information without cluttering the main document.

2.2.2 Purpose and Importance of SRS

1. **Question: What is the primary purpose of a Software Requirement Specification (SRS)?**
   Answer: The primary purpose of an SRS is to provide a detailed and unambiguous description of what a software system must accomplish. It serves as a crucial reference for all stakeholders, ensuring a shared understanding of the project's goals and requirements.

2. **Question: Why is it important to create an SRS at the beginning of a software project?**
   Answer: Creating an SRS at the project's outset is vital because it sets the foundation for the entire development process. It helps in avoiding misunderstandings, scope creep, and costly changes later on, ensuring the project stays on track.

3. **Question: How does an SRS benefit project managers and development teams?**
   Answer: An SRS provides a clear roadmap for project managers to plan and track the project's progress. For development teams, it serves as a blueprint, reducing ambiguity, improving collaboration, and guiding the implementation process.

4. **Question: In what ways does an SRS support effective communication between project stakeholders?**
   Answer: An SRS acts as a common language for stakeholders, including developers, testers, designers, and clients. It ensures that everyone involved shares a common understanding of the project's requirements and objectives.

5. **Question: What role does an SRS play in risk management during software development?**
Answer: An SRS helps identify potential risks and challenges early in the project, allowing for proactive risk mitigation. It aids in minimizing misunderstandings and errors that can lead to costly rework or project delays.

2.2.3 Parts of SRS

1. **Question: What are the key components or parts typically found in an SRS document?**
Answer: An SRS document commonly consists of several parts, including the Introduction, Purpose, Scope, Functional Requirements, Non-Functional Requirements, System Architecture, User Interface, and Appendices.

2. **Question: Why is the Introduction section an essential part of an SRS?**
Answer: The Introduction provides an overview of the software project, explaining its context, purpose, scope, and intended audience. It serves as a starting point for understanding the document.

3. **Question: What is the significance of the Functional Requirements section in an SRS?**
Answer: The Functional Requirements section details the specific functions, features, and behaviors the software must exhibit. It describes how the software should work, including use cases, scenarios, and user interactions.

4. **Question: How do Non-Functional Requirements differ from Functional Requirements in an SRS?**
Answer: Non-Functional Requirements focus on aspects like performance, security, usability, and scalability. They specify the quality attributes and constraints that the software must meet or adhere to.

5. **Question: What role does the Appendices section play in an SRS, and what kind of information might be included there?**
Answer: The Appendices section contains supplementary information such as data dictionaries, sample mockups, or technical details that can be referenced for more in-depth information without cluttering the main document.

2.2.4 Classification of Software Requirement

1. **Question: How are software requirements typically classified, and why is this classification important?**
Answer: Software requirements are commonly classified into two categories: Functional Requirements and Non-Functional Requirements. This classification is important because it helps distinguish what the software must do (functional) from how it should do it (non-functional).

2. **Question: Can you explain Functional Requirements and provide an example?**
Answer: Functional Requirements specify the specific functions and features the software should perform. An example might be, "The system shall allow users to log in using a username and password."

3. **Question: What are Non-Functional Requirements, and why are they crucial in software development?**
Answer: Non-Functional Requirements define the quality attributes and constraints the software must adhere to, such as performance, security, or usability. They are crucial because they determine how well the software functions in various aspects beyond its core functionality.

4. **Question: How are Requirements categorized in terms of their source of origin?**
Answer: Requirements can be categorized based on their source as User Requirements, System Requirements, and Stakeholder Requirements. User Requirements originate from end-users, System Requirements are technical specifications, and Stakeholder Requirements come from various project stakeholders.

5. **Question: What is the distinction between High-Level and Low-Level Requirements in terms of classification?**
Answer: High-Level Requirements, often called Business Requirements, describe the overall goals and objectives of the software system. Low-Level Requirements, or Detailed Requirements, break these high-level goals into specific, detailed functions, and features.

2.2.5 Quality characteristics of a good SRS

1. **Question: What are the key quality characteristics that define a good SRS document?**
   Answer: A good SRS document exhibits several essential quality characteristics, including Clarity, Completeness, Consistency, Verifiability, and Traceability.

2. **Question: Why is Clarity an important quality characteristic in an SRS?**
   Answer: Clarity ensures that the requirements are easy to understand for all stakeholders, reducing the potential for misunderstandings or misinterpretations.

3. **Question: What does Completeness mean in the context of an SRS, and why is it crucial?**
   Answer: Completeness means that all necessary requirements are included. It's crucial to avoid gaps in the project scope that could lead to costly changes or project delays.

4. **Question: How does Consistency enhance the quality of an SRS?**
   Answer: Consistency ensures that the requirements within the document do not conflict with each other. A consistent SRS prevents confusion and reduces the risk of errors during development.

5. **Question: Explain the significance of Verifiability and Traceability as quality characteristics in an SRS.**
   Answer: Verifiability means that each requirement can be tested to confirm its correctness, while Traceability ensures that each requirement is linked back to its source. Both characteristics are critical for validation and change management.

Online Resources

Chapter 2 YouTube Playlist Link:
Link: https://www.youtube.com/playlist?list=PLzlh_31VWEFpO9Cc5Av_iP4FUcMcYXlWG
QR Code:

Online Exam Paper Link:
Link: https://forms.gle/mz1EaJuePRyzUVhj6
QR Code:

MCQ Video Playlist Link:
Link: https://youtu.be/G2XcypVTWls
QR Code:

True/False Video Playlist Link:
Link: https://youtu.be/UkGrYHgfd_8
QR Code:

Online MCQ Exam Paper Link:
Link: https://forms.office.com/r/mRwQtBTatc
QR Code:

Online True/False Exam Paper Link:
Link: https://forms.office.com/r/McCWAytvmp
QR Code:

Chapter 3: Software Measurement and metrics

3.1 Introduction of Software Measurement and Metrics

1. **Question: What is the basic concept of Software Measurement and Metrics?**
   Answer: Software Measurement and Metrics involve quantifying software attributes to assess its quality, performance, and other characteristics. It provides a data-driven approach to managing and improving software development processes.

2. **Question: Why is Software Measurement and Metrics important in software development?**
   Answer: Software Measurement and Metrics provide objective data that helps in making informed decisions, tracking progress, identifying areas for improvement, and ultimately enhancing the quality, productivity, and efficiency of software development.

3. **Question: Can you explain the distinction between software measurement and software metrics?**
   Answer: Software measurement is the process of quantifying software attributes, while software metrics are the actual measurements or data points collected during the measurement process. Metrics are the concrete values, while measurement is the act of obtaining those values.

4. **Question: What are some common categories of software metrics?**
   Answer: Common categories of software metrics include product metrics (assessing the software itself), process metrics (evaluating the development process), and project metrics (focused on project management aspects).

5. **Question: How can software measurement and metrics benefit an organization's software development practices?**
   Answer: Software measurement and metrics provide an objective basis for evaluating and improving software development processes. They help in identifying bottlenecks, predicting project outcomes, and driving continuous process improvement.

3.2 People Metrics and Process Metrics

1. **Question: What are People Metrics in software development, and why are they important?**
   Answer: People Metrics focus on the performance, productivity, and efficiency of the individuals or teams involved in software development. They are crucial for assessing and optimizing the human resources aspect of the development process.

2. **Question: Can you provide examples of People Metrics used in software development?**
   Answer: Examples of People Metrics include individual or team productivity measurements, code contribution and quality, time spent on tasks, defect resolution rates, and employee satisfaction surveys.

3. **Question: What do Process Metrics in software development aim to measure, and how do they benefit the development process?**
   Answer: Process Metrics assess the effectiveness and efficiency of the development process itself. They help in identifying areas for improvement, optimizing workflows, and enhancing the overall quality and predictability of software development.

4. **Question: What are some common Process Metrics used in software development projects?**
   Answer: Common Process Metrics include cycle time (the time taken to complete a task or process), defect density (the number of defects per unit of code), lead time (the time from the start to completion of a task), and change request rate (the frequency of change requests during development).

5. **Question: How can the combination of People Metrics and Process Metrics contribute to successful software development projects?**

Answer: By combining People Metrics and Process Metrics, organizations can assess the performance of both individuals and teams and evaluate the effectiveness of development processes. This holistic approach enables data-driven decision-making, continuous improvement, and the delivery of high-quality software products.

3.3 Cyclomatic Complexity

1. **Question: What is Cyclomatic Complexity in software development?**
   Answer: Cyclomatic Complexity is a software metric used to quantify the complexity of a program's control flow, helping in understanding its testability and potential for errors.

2. **Question: Why is Cyclomatic Complexity important in software quality assessment?**
   Answer: Cyclomatic Complexity is crucial because it aids in identifying areas of code that might be more error-prone, challenging to test, or require refactoring to improve code maintainability and quality.

3. **Question: How is Cyclomatic Complexity calculated, and what does a higher value signify?**
   Answer: Cyclomatic Complexity is calculated by counting the number of independent paths through a program's control flow graph. A higher value indicates increased program complexity and a potentially higher testing effort.

4. **Question: What is the significance of reducing Cyclomatic Complexity in software projects?**
   Answer: Reducing Cyclomatic Complexity is important as it leads to code that is easier to understand, test, and maintain. Lower complexity often correlates with fewer bugs and enhanced software reliability.

5. **Question: Can you provide an example of how Cyclomatic Complexity is used in practice to improve software quality?**
   Answer: Sure, Cyclomatic Complexity can help identify complex and convoluted sections of code. Developers can then refactor these areas to make them more modular and easier to test, resulting in code that is more reliable and maintainable.

3.4 Functional Point Analysis

1. **Question: What is Functional Point Analysis (FPA) in software development?**
   Answer: Functional Point Analysis (FPA) is a structured method for quantifying the functionality provided by a software application. It helps in measuring the size and complexity of software systems based on the user's perspective.

2. **Question: Why is Functional Point Analysis important in software project estimation?**
   Answer: FPA is vital for software project estimation because it provides a standardized way to measure the software's functional requirements. This helps in creating more accurate project schedules, resource allocation, and cost estimates.

3. **Question: How are functional points calculated, and what are the components considered in the calculation?**
   Answer: Functional Points are calculated by quantifying five components: External Inputs, External Outputs, External Inquiries, Internal Logical Files, and External Interface Files. These components capture the interactions between users and the software.

4. **Question: What are the benefits of using Functional Point Analysis for software projects?**
   Answer: FPA offers several benefits, including objective measurement of software size, better project planning, improved communication between stakeholders, and the ability to compare software productivity across different projects.

5. **Question: How does Functional Point Analysis adapt to agile development methodologies, which emphasize change and iterative development?**
   Answer: FPA can be adapted for agile methodologies by adjusting the count of functional points as the software evolves. Each iteration can result in new functionality being added, modified, or removed, allowing for more flexibility and accurate measurement in agile environments.

3.5 Line of code (LOC)

1. **Question: What is Lines of Code (LOC) in software development?**
   Answer: Lines of Code (LOC) is a metric used to quantify the number of lines in a source code file. It's often used to measure code size, complexity, and productivity.

2. **Question: Why is LOC used as a metric in software development, and what can it indicate about a software project?**
   Answer: LOC is used to assess code size, estimate development effort, and evaluate code maintainability. It can indicate the scale of a project, but it doesn't provide a comprehensive measure of software quality or functionality.

3. **Question: Are there any limitations or challenges associated with using LOC as a metric in software development?**
   Answer: Yes, LOC has limitations as it doesn't account for differences in programming languages, coding styles, or code quality. Additionally, it can be misleading in cases where a few lines of code accomplish significant functionality, or in projects using code generation tools.

4. **Question: How can LOC be used to estimate project effort, and what factors should be considered when making such estimates?**
   Answer: LOC can be used for high-level effort estimation by comparing it to historical data. However, factors such as team experience, code complexity, and technology choices should also be considered for more accurate effort estimates.

5. **Question: What are some alternatives or complementary metrics to LOC that provide a more comprehensive view of software quality and development progress?**
   Answer: Alternatives to LOC include function points, Cyclomatic Complexity, and code review metrics. These metrics offer more insight into software quality, complexity, and maintainability, complementing LOC as a measure of code size.

Online Resources

Chapter 3 YouTube Playlist Link:
Link: https://www.youtube.com/playlist?list=PLzlh_31VWEFrArOJ-tZRk9Ex3SOWzFog1
QR Code:

Online Exam Paper Link:
Link: https://forms.gle/6YsnrqWfAMvtkLgVA
QR Code:

MCQ Video Playlist Link:
Link: https://youtu.be/qV2i1M1MeyI
QR Code:

True/False Video Playlist Link:
Link: https://youtu.be/8Box9X3hgDo
QR Code:

Online MCQ Exam Paper Link:
Link: https://forms.office.com/r/rv0aYmetuF
QR Code:

Online True/False Exam Paper Link:
Link: https://forms.office.com/r/B8n6zN5BsG
QR Code:

Chapter 4: Software Development Models

4.1 Classical Waterfall Model

1. Question: What is the Classical Waterfall Model in software development?
Answer: The Classical Waterfall Model is a linear and sequential software development approach where each phase of the project follows the previous one in a cascading manner, without overlapping or iteration.

2. Question: Can you describe the typical phases of the Classical Waterfall Model?
Answer: The Classical Waterfall Model consists of distinct phases, including Requirements, Design, Implementation, Testing, Deployment, and Maintenance, each building upon the results of the preceding phase.

3. Question: What are the advantages of using the Classical Waterfall Model in software projects?
Answer: Advantages of the Waterfall Model include its simplicity, clear documentation at each phase, and suitability for well-defined projects with stable requirements.

4. Question: What are the limitations or challenges associated with the Classical Waterfall Model?
Answer: Challenges include limited adaptability to changing requirements, lack of customer involvement until late in the project, and potential for costly rework if issues arise late in the development cycle.

5. Question: In which scenarios is the Classical Waterfall Model a suitable choice for software development projects?
Answer: The Classical Waterfall Model is best suited for projects with well-understood, stable requirements, where the cost of change is high. It's often used in fields like defense, aerospace, and some large-scale infrastructure projects.

4.2 Iterative waterfall Model

1. Question: What is the Iterative Waterfall Model in software development, and how does it differ from the traditional Waterfall Model?
Answer: The Iterative Waterfall Model is an extension of the traditional Waterfall Model. It introduces iterations, allowing for feedback and adjustments between phases, making it more flexible and responsive to changing requirements.

2. Question: Can you explain the concept of iterations in the Iterative Waterfall Model?
Answer: In the Iterative Waterfall Model, the development process is divided into multiple cycles or iterations. Each iteration goes through the traditional Waterfall phases (Requirements, Design, Implementation, Testing), and after each iteration, feedback is used to refine and improve the product.

3. Question: What are the advantages of using the Iterative Waterfall Model over the traditional Waterfall Model?
Answer: The Iterative Waterfall Model offers benefits like increased flexibility, faster response to changes, and the ability to incorporate user feedback earlier in the development process, resulting in a more adaptable and refined final product.

4. Question: What challenges or potential drawbacks may be associated with the Iterative Waterfall Model?
Answer: Challenges include the need for effective project management to coordinate multiple iterations and the risk of scope creep if not managed carefully. Additionally, it may not be the best choice for projects with very stable and well-defined requirements.

5. Question: In which scenarios is the Iterative Waterfall Model a suitable choice for software development projects?
Answer: The Iterative Waterfall Model is a good fit for projects where some flexibility is needed but where a more controlled and structured approach is still required. It's often used in projects with moderately stable requirements

4.3 Spiral Model

1. **Question: What is the Spiral Model in software development, and how does it differ from other software development models like Waterfall?**
   Answer: The Spiral Model is a risk-driven software development process that combines elements of iterative development and prototyping with risk assessment and management. Unlike the Waterfall model, it allows for iterative cycles and risk analysis in each phase.

2. **Question: Can you explain the key phases of the Spiral Model and how they are organized?**
   Answer: The Spiral Model consists of four main phases: Planning, Risk Analysis, Engineering, and Evaluation. These phases are organized into a spiral pattern, with each loop representing a cycle of development.

3. **Question: What is the primary objective of the Risk Analysis phase in the Spiral Model?**
   Answer: The Risk Analysis phase aims to identify, assess, and mitigate potential risks associated with the project. It helps in making informed decisions about the project's direction and ensures that risks are addressed early in the development process.

4. **Question: What are the advantages of using the Spiral Model in software development?**
   Answer: The Spiral Model offers benefits such as risk management, early identification of issues, flexibility in accommodating changes, and the ability to build and refine a high-quality product.

5. **Question: What are some examples of software projects or industries where the Spiral Model is commonly employed?**
   Answer: The Spiral Model is often used in complex software projects, especially in fields like aerospace, defense, healthcare, and critical systems development, where risk management and thorough testing are paramount. It's also useful for projects with evolving or unclear requirements.

4.4 Prototyping Model

1. **Question: What is the Prototyping Model in software development, and how does it differ from other software development models like Waterfall?**
   Answer: The Prototyping Model is an iterative software development approach where a preliminary version of the software is created to visualize and validate requirements. Unlike the Waterfall model, it emphasizes user involvement and early feedback.

2. **Question: How does the Prototyping Model work, and what is the purpose of the prototype in the development process?**
   Answer: In the Prototyping Model, a basic version of the software is developed to help stakeholders understand and refine their requirements. The prototype serves as a visual aid for better communication and helps identify potential issues early in the project.

3. **Question: What are the advantages of using the Prototyping Model in software development?**
   Answer: The Prototyping Model offers advantages such as enhanced requirement clarity, improved user satisfaction, reduced development risks, and increased flexibility to adapt to changing requirements.

4. **Question: Are there any challenges or limitations associated with the Prototyping Model?**
   Answer: Challenges may include difficulties in managing and documenting multiple iterations, the risk of scope creep, and the potential for misunderstandings if stakeholders confuse the prototype with the final product.

5. **Question: In which scenarios is the Prototyping Model a suitable choice for software development projects?**
   Answer: The Prototyping Model is particularly suitable for projects with evolving or unclear requirements, where a close collaboration with end-users is essential. It's often used in web and mobile app development, as well as user interface design and other interactive systems.

4.5 Incremental Process Model

1. **Question: What is the Incremental Process Model in software development, and how does it differ from the traditional Waterfall model?**
   Answer: The Incremental Process Model is an iterative approach where the software is developed in increments or pieces. Unlike the Waterfall model, it allows for partial system development and delivery in stages.

2. **Question: Can you explain how the development process is organized in the Incremental Process Model?**
   Answer: In the Incremental Process Model, the software is divided into smaller, manageable parts or increments. Each increment is developed separately and integrates with the previously developed increments.

3. **Question: What is the primary advantage of using the Incremental Process Model in software development?**
   Answer: The primary advantage is that it enables early delivery of a functional part of the software, which allows users to start utilizing and providing feedback on it sooner. This can lead to better alignment with user needs and requirements.

4. **Question: Are there any challenges or potential drawbacks associated with the Incremental Process Model?**
   Answer: Challenges include ensuring smooth integration of increments, maintaining a well-organized development plan, and addressing potential inconsistencies that may arise as different parts of the software are developed incrementally.

5. **Question: In which scenarios is the Incremental Process Model a suitable choice for software development projects?**
   Answer: The Incremental Process Model is suitable for projects where early delivery of functional software is required, and where the project can be logically divided into increments. It's commonly used in web development, large systems, and projects with evolving requirements or ongoing improvements.

4.6 Rapid Application Development Model (RAD)

1. **Question: What is the Rapid Application Development (RAD) Model in software development, and how does it differ from traditional models like Waterfall?**
   Answer: The RAD Model is an iterative and incremental development approach that prioritizes rapid prototyping and user feedback. Unlike the Waterfall model, it aims to deliver a functioning application quickly and incrementally.

2. **Question: Can you explain the core principles of RAD and how it speeds up the development process?**
   Answer: RAD focuses on rapid prototyping, parallel development, and strong user involvement. It speeds up development by quickly creating working prototypes that allow users to provide feedback and refine requirements early in the process.

3. **Question: What are the key advantages of using the RAD Model in software development?**
   Answer: Advantages of RAD include rapid development, better user involvement, improved adaptability to changing requirements, and the ability to create functional systems quickly.

4. **Question: Are there any challenges or limitations associated with the RAD Model?**
   Answer: Challenges may include the need for skilled personnel, difficulties in managing large projects, and potential concerns about the depth of analysis in the early stages of development.

5. **Question: In which scenarios is the RAD Model a suitable choice for software development projects?**
   Answer: RAD is often chosen for projects with well-defined user requirements, short timeframes, and a need for early functionality. It's particularly useful for web and mobile app development, where user interface and user experience are critical.

4.7 V-Model

1. **Question: What is the V-Model in software development, and how does it differ from the traditional Waterfall model?**

Answer: The V-Model, or Verification and Validation Model, is an extension of the Waterfall model. It emphasizes the parallel testing and verification of each development phase, resulting in a V-shaped diagram that illustrates the relationship between development and testing activities.

2. **Question: Can you explain the key concept behind the V-Model and how it helps ensure software quality?**
   Answer: The key concept is that each development phase corresponds to a testing phase on the other side of the V. This approach ensures that each requirement is thoroughly tested, leading to higher software quality.

3. **Question: What are the advantages of using the V-Model in software development projects?**
   Answer: Advantages of the V-Model include improved quality through early verification, well-defined and traceable requirements, and a clear mapping of testing activities to development phases.

4. **Question: Are there any challenges or limitations associated with the V-Model?**
   Answer: Challenges may include the need for detailed and well-defined requirements upfront, which can be challenging in projects with evolving or uncertain requirements. It can also be less flexible than some other models for accommodating changes.
5. **Question: In which scenarios is the V-Model a suitable choice for software development projects?**
   Answer: The V-Model is suitable for projects with stable and well-understood requirements, where thorough verification and validation are essential, such as in safety-critical systems like aerospace, healthcare, and automotive industries.

Online Resources

Chapter 4 YouTube Playlist Link:
Link: https://www.youtube.com/playlist?list=PLzlh_31VWEFps2eNLdR36zxZZ2UnXiMb3
QR Code:

Online Exam Paper Link:
Link: https://forms.gle/TtW5VP7VzkMbraPr8
QR Code:

MCQ Video Playlist Link:
Link: https://youtu.be/6Hd4IBevKWM
QR Code:

True/False Video Playlist Link:
Link: https://youtu.be/fTND_yCPlNk
QR Code:

Online MCQ Exam Paper Link:
Link: https://forms.office.com/r/7F66kujXEL
QR Code:

Online True/False Exam Paper Link:
Link: https://forms.office.com/r/XQ6p6nu6G6
QR Code:

Chapter 5: Agile Software Development

5.1 Introduction Agile Software Development

1. Question: What is Agile Software Development, and how does it differ from traditional development methodologies?
Answer: Agile Software Development is an iterative and flexible approach that values collaboration, customer feedback, and responding to change. It differs from traditional methods by emphasizing adaptability and delivering working software in short, incremental iterations.

2. Question: Can you describe the core values and principles of Agile development, as outlined in the Agile Manifesto?
Answer: The Agile Manifesto emphasizes values such as individuals and interactions over processes and tools, working software over comprehensive documentation, customer collaboration over contract negotiation, and responding to change over following a plan.

3. Question: What is the significance of user stories in Agile development, and how are they used to capture requirements?
Answer: User stories are concise, user-centric descriptions of software functionality. They are used in Agile to capture and prioritize requirements, ensuring that development efforts focus on delivering value to end-users.

4. Question: How does Agile development foster close collaboration between development teams and stakeholders, and why is this collaboration important?
Answer: Agile encourages regular interactions between teams and stakeholders, including customers. This collaboration ensures that the software aligns with user needs, and it allows for feedback and adjustments throughout the development process, leading to a more customer-centric product.

5. Question: In what types of projects or industries is Agile Software Development commonly applied?
Answer: Agile is applied across various industries and project types, including software development, web and mobile app development, product development, and even non-software projects where adaptability and incremental progress are essential. It is especially well-suited for projects with evolving or unclear requirements.

5.2 Agile Development Models

1. Question: What are Agile Development Models, and how do they differ from traditional development models?
Answer: Agile Development Models are a set of iterative and flexible approaches to software development that prioritize adaptability and collaboration. They differ from traditional models by embracing change, delivering working software incrementally, and fostering customer involvement throughout the project.

2. Question: Can you name some popular Agile Development Models and briefly explain their key characteristics?
Answer: Some popular Agile models include Scrum, Kanban, and Extreme Programming (XP). Scrum emphasizes time-boxed development cycles and roles like Product Owner and Scrum Master. Kanban focuses on visualizing work and optimizing flow. XP promotes coding practices, continuous integration, and customer involvement.

3. Question: What role does the Agile Manifesto play in shaping Agile Development Models, and what are its key values and principles?
Answer: The Agile Manifesto is a foundational document that highlights values such as individuals and interactions, working software, customer collaboration, and responding to change. Its principles prioritize customer satisfaction, delivering value, and embracing change.

4. Question: How does Agile Development accommodate changing requirements and priorities, and why is this adaptability important?

Answer: Agile processes are designed to handle changing requirements by allowing adjustments at the end of each iteration. This adaptability is crucial because it ensures that the software remains aligned with evolving user needs and market conditions.

5. **Question: In which scenarios are Agile Development Models a suitable choice for software development projects, and what are their key benefits?**
   Answer: Agile models are well-suited for projects with evolving or unclear requirements, as well as those where customer feedback and adaptability are paramount. Their key benefits include faster time-to-market, improved collaboration, and the ability to deliver a product that better meets user expectations.

5.3 Advantages and Disadvantages of Agile Methodology

1. **Question: What are some key advantages of using the Agile methodology in software development?**
   Answer: Agile offers advantages like faster time-to-market, improved customer satisfaction, adaptability to changing requirements, increased collaboration, and a focus on delivering working software in short iterations.

2. **Question: Can you explain how Agile promotes customer collaboration, and why is this an advantage?**
   Answer: Agile encourages regular interactions with customers, involving them in the development process. This advantage helps ensure the software aligns with customer needs, reducing the risk of misalignment or surprises at project completion.

3. **Question: What are some disadvantages or challenges associated with implementing Agile in software projects?**
   Answer: Disadvantages include difficulties in managing scope, the potential for scope creep, the need for highly skilled team members, and the challenge of adhering to project timelines.

4. **Question: How does Agile handle changing requirements, and what are the potential drawbacks of this adaptability?**
   Answer: Agile accommodates changing requirements through iterative development. However, the drawback is that uncontrolled changes can lead to project delays, scope issues, or difficulties in maintaining a stable development pace.

5. **Question: In which types of projects or scenarios is Agile well-suited, and when might other methodologies be more appropriate?**
   Answer: Agile is well-suited for projects with evolving or unclear requirements, customer-driven development, and the need for rapid iterations. Other methodologies, like Waterfall, might be more appropriate for projects with highly stable and well-defined requirements, where strict planning and documentation are necessary.

5.4 Agile Software Development Life Cycle

1. **Question: What is the Agile Software Development Life Cycle, and how does it differ from the traditional Waterfall model?**
   Answer: The Agile Software Development Life Cycle is an iterative approach that focuses on incremental development, collaboration, and delivering working software in short cycles. It differs from the Waterfall model by its adaptability, flexibility, and continuous customer involvement.

2. **Question: Can you describe the typical phases of the Agile Software Development Life Cycle?**
   Answer: The Agile Life Cycle typically includes phases like project initiation, requirement gathering, sprint planning, iterative development, daily stand-ups, testing, and sprint review and retrospective, followed by continuous delivery and maintenance.

3. **Question: How does Agile handle project planning and adapt to changing requirements throughout the development process?**
   Answer: Agile uses iterative planning, allowing project teams to adjust priorities and requirements after each iteration. This adaptability ensures that the project remains aligned with evolving user needs and market conditions.

4. **Question: What role does continuous testing and customer feedback play in the Agile Software Development Life Cycle, and why are they important?**
   Answer: Continuous testing and customer feedback are integral to Agile. They help identify issues early, ensure the software meets user expectations, and provide a mechanism for refining requirements and delivering high-quality products.

5. **Question: In which scenarios is the Agile Software Development Life Cycle a suitable choice for software development projects, and what are its key benefits?**
   Answer: Agile is suitable for projects with evolving or unclear requirements, where customer feedback, rapid iterations, and adaptability are essential. Its benefits include faster time-to-market, improved collaboration, and a focus on delivering value to end-users.

Online Resources

Chapter 5 YouTube Playlist Link:
Link: https://www.youtube.com/playlist?list=PLzlh_31VWEFqcHMJdHsQm1NxsE0ugxVik
QR Code:

Online Exam Paper Link:
Link: https://forms.gle/BtnHAWwazUtjDBPp7
QR Code:

MCQ Video Playlist Link:
Link: https://youtu.be/QdMvnIHstEE
QR Code:

True/False Video Playlist Link:
Link: https://youtu.be/SDOC2s9zXlg
QR Code:

Online MCQ Exam Paper Link:
Link: https://forms.office.com/r/gxYQ6AkP0u
QR Code:

Online True/False Exam Paper Link:
Link: https://forms.office.com/r/z17wvn6qTP
QR Code:

Chapter 6: Software Design

6.1 Software Design Introduction

1. **Question: What is Software Design, and why is it a crucial phase in the software development process?**
   Answer: Software Design is the process of defining the structure, architecture, and components of a software system. It's a critical phase because it lays the foundation for the implementation, ensuring that the software meets its functional and non-functional requirements.

2. **Question: Can you explain the difference between High-Level Design and Low-Level Design in software development?**
   Answer: High-Level Design focuses on the overall structure and architecture of the software, while Low-Level Design delves into the specifics of individual components, algorithms, and data structures. High-Level Design sets the system's structure, and Low-Level Design defines the internal workings.

3. **Question: How does Software Design contribute to software quality and maintainability?**
   Answer: Good Software Design practices result in software that is easier to maintain, understand, and extend. It also helps in reducing the likelihood of defects and improves the overall quality of the software.

4. **Question: What are some common design principles and patterns that software designers use to guide their work?**
   Answer: Common principles include SOLID principles (Single Responsibility, Open-Closed, Liskov Substitution, Interface Segregation, and Dependency Inversion). Design patterns such as the Singleton, Factory, and Observer patterns are also frequently used.

5. **Question: How does Software Design involve trade-offs between various factors like performance, maintainability, and cost?**
   Answer: Software Design involves making decisions that balance trade-offs between factors like performance, maintainability, cost, and time-to-market. Designers must weigh these factors to make informed choices that align with project goals and priorities.

6.2 Design Process

1. **Question: What is the Design Process in software development, and why is it important?**
   Answer: The Design Process involves creating a detailed plan for the software's structure, components, and functionality. It's essential because it bridges the gap between requirements and implementation, ensuring that the software meets user needs and quality standards.

2. **Question: Can you describe the key steps involved in the Design Process?**
   Answer: The Design Process typically includes steps like architectural design, detailed design, interface design, and database design. These steps help create a blueprint for the software's construction.

3. **Question: How does the Design Process facilitate communication and collaboration among project stakeholders?**
   Answer: The Design Process creates visual representations and documentation that serve as a common language for developers, testers, and business stakeholders. This facilitates effective communication and alignment of project objectives.

4. **Question: What role do design principles and patterns play in the Design Process, and how do they enhance the quality of software?**
   Answer: Design principles and patterns guide designers in making sound design decisions. They promote maintainability, extensibility, and code reusability, leading to high-quality, efficient software.

5. **Question: In what ways can the Design Process impact the overall success of a software project, and what challenges may arise during the design phase?**

Answer: Effective design can lead to a successful project by ensuring that the software is well-structured, efficient, and meets user needs. Challenges during design include balancing trade-offs, managing complexity, and ensuring that the design aligns with project constraints and goals.

6.3 Software Design Models

1. **Question: What are Software Design Models, and why are they used in software development?**
Answer: Software Design Models are abstract representations of a software system's structure, components, and interactions. They are used to plan and communicate the design of the software, helping ensure that it meets its functional and non-functional requirements.

2. **Question: Can you explain the difference between Structural Models and Behavioral Models in software design?**
Answer: Structural Models focus on the system's architecture and components, while Behavioral Models describe how the system's components interact to achieve functionality. Structural models provide a static view, while behavioral models provide a dynamic view of the software.

3. **Question: What are some common Software Design Models and their key characteristics?**
Answer: Common design models include the UML (Unified Modeling Language), Data Flow Diagrams (DFD), Entity-Relationship Diagrams (ERD), and State Transition Diagrams. Each model serves specific purposes, from visualizing system architecture to illustrating data flow and interactions.

4. **Question: How do Software Design Models aid in the development process and in the creation of high-quality software?**
Answer: Design models help in visualizing and planning the software's structure, guiding the development team, and ensuring alignment with user requirements. They also enhance the understanding of the software's architecture and support efficient communication among project stakeholders.

5. **Question: In which scenarios or projects are specific Software Design Models more suitable, and how can their selection impact the success of a project?**
Answer: The choice of design model depends on the project's requirements and complexity. UML, for example, is widely used for modeling software architecture and design, while DFDs are valuable for understanding data flow. Selecting the appropriate model is crucial as it can greatly impact project clarity, quality, and success.

6.4 General Design Process

1. **Question: What is the General Design Process in software development, and why is it important?**
Answer: The General Design Process is the systematic approach to creating a detailed plan for a software system's architecture, components, and functionality. It's crucial because it bridges the gap between high-level requirements and the actual implementation, ensuring that the software meets user needs and quality standards.

2. **Question: Can you describe the key steps typically involved in the General Design Process?**
Answer: The General Design Process typically includes steps like architectural design, detailed design, interface design, and database design. These steps are essential for creating a comprehensive blueprint for the software's construction.

3. **Question: How does the General Design Process facilitate collaboration and effective communication among development teams and stakeholders?**
Answer: The General Design Process involves creating visual representations and documentation, serving as a common language for developers, testers, and business stakeholders. This enables effective communication, alignment of objectives, and a shared understanding of the software's structure and functionality.

4. **Question: What role do design principles and patterns play in the General Design Process, and how do they enhance the quality and maintainability of software?**

Answer: Design principles and patterns guide designers in making sound decisions. They promote good software design practices, including maintainability, scalability, and code reusability, leading to high-quality and efficient software.

5. **Question: In what ways can the General Design Process impact the overall success of a software project, and what challenges may arise during the design phase?**
   Answer: The General Design Process plays a critical role in project success by ensuring that the software is well-structured, efficient, and aligned with user needs. Challenges during design can include balancing trade-offs, managing complexity, and aligning the design with project constraints and goals.

6.5 Software Design Process

1. **Question: What is the Software Design Process, and why is it a crucial phase in software development?**
   Answer: The Software Design Process is the systematic approach to defining the architecture, components, and functionality of a software system. It's critical because it bridges the gap between high-level requirements and implementation, ensuring the software aligns with user needs and quality standards.

2. **Question: Can you explain the key steps involved in the Software Design Process?**
   Answer: The Software Design Process generally includes architectural design, detailed design, interface design, and database design. These steps help create a detailed blueprint for the software's construction.

3. **Question: How does the Software Design Process promote collaboration and effective communication among development teams and stakeholders?**
   Answer: The process involves creating visual representations and documentation, which serve as a common language for developers, testers, and business stakeholders. This facilitates effective communication, alignment of project goals, and a shared understanding of the software's structure and functionality.

4. **Question: What role do design principles and patterns play in the Software Design Process, and how do they contribute to software quality?**
   Answer: Design principles and patterns guide designers in making informed decisions, promoting software quality, maintainability, and scalability. They ensure that the software is well-structured and efficient.

5. **Question: In what ways can the Software Design Process impact the overall success of a software project, and what challenges may arise during the design phase?**
   Answer: The Software Design Process significantly affects project success by ensuring the software aligns with user needs, is well-structured, and efficient. Challenges may include managing complexity, balancing trade-offs, and aligning the design with project constraints and goals.

6.6 Software design Strategies

1. **Question: What are software design strategies, and why are they important in software development?**
   Answer: Software design strategies are high-level approaches to solving design problems in software development. They are crucial because they guide designers in making informed decisions that impact the quality, efficiency, and maintainability of the software.

2. **Question: Can you describe some common software design strategies and their use cases?**
   Answer: Common design strategies include modular design for creating cohesive and loosely coupled modules, layered design for separating concerns, and design patterns like the Singleton pattern for ensuring a single instance of a class.

3. **Question: How do software design strategies contribute to code reusability, and why is reusability important?**
   Answer: Software design strategies encourage the creation of reusable components and patterns, reducing redundancy and promoting efficient development. Reusability is essential because it saves time, maintains consistency, and reduces the likelihood of errors.

4. Question: What role does simplicity play in software design strategies, and how does it impact the quality of software?
Answer: Simplicity is a key principle in many design strategies. It promotes clarity, reduces complexity, and enhances code maintainability. Simple designs are easier to understand, modify, and troubleshoot.

5. Question: In which scenarios are specific software design strategies more suitable, and how can their selection impact the success of a project?
Answer: The choice of design strategy depends on the project's specific requirements and constraints. Selecting the appropriate strategy can significantly impact a project's success by ensuring that the software is well-structured, efficient, and aligned with its objectives and scope.

6.7 Algorithms and Its Characteristics

1. Question: What is an algorithm, and why is it fundamental in computer science and software development?
Answer: An algorithm is a well-defined set of steps for solving a specific problem or performing a task. Algorithms are fundamental because they enable computers to process data, make decisions, and perform complex tasks efficiently.

2. Question: What are the key characteristics of a good algorithm?
Answer: Good algorithms are characterized by correctness, efficiency, clarity, and adaptability. They should produce the correct output, be resource-efficient, easy to understand, and capable of adapting to changing input data.

3. Question: How does the efficiency of an algorithm relate to factors like time complexity and space complexity?
Answer: Efficiency is often measured by an algorithm's time and space complexity. Time complexity indicates how the algorithm's runtime scales with input size, while space complexity indicates how its memory usage scales. Good algorithms aim to minimize both.

4. Question: Can you explain the concept of algorithmic correctness and the importance of thorough testing in algorithm development?
Answer: Algorithmic correctness means the algorithm produces the desired output for all possible valid inputs. Thorough testing is crucial to verify correctness, ensuring that the algorithm behaves as expected under various conditions.

5. Question: In what real-world scenarios are algorithms applied, and how do they impact software and technology as a whole?
Answer: Algorithms are applied in various scenarios, from search engines and recommendation systems to data analysis and cryptography. They have a profound impact on technology, enabling the development of efficient and intelligent software solutions that drive innovation and progress.

Online Resources

Chapter 6 YouTube Playlist Link:
Link: https://www.youtube.com/playlist?list=PLzlh_31VWEFoE6zOQD-kGLWJZ65MuTrZz
QR Code:

Online Exam Paper Link:
Link: https://forms.gle/izvs2KyBVkypN5Mx5
QR Code:

MCQ Video Playlist Link:
Link: https://youtu.be/-3eVGJFGyQ8
QR Code:

True/False Video Playlist Link:
Link: https://youtu.be/OJEY_Cpnoiw
QR Code:

Online MCQ Exam Paper Link:
Link: https://forms.office.com/r/LbpFgH9KK3
QR Code:

Online True/False Exam Paper Link:
Link: https://forms.office.com/r/YyPxv8LNpM
QR Code:

Chapter 7: Design Principles

7.1 Design Objectives

Question 1: What are the primary design objectives in software development?
Answer: The primary design objectives in software development are functionality, performance, usability, scalability, and maintainability. These objectives ensure that the software meets user needs, performs efficiently, is user-friendly, can handle growing workloads, and is easy to maintain and update.

Question 2: Why is functionality a crucial design objective in software development?
Answer: Functionality is a critical design objective because it ensures that the software performs the intended tasks and meets user requirements. Designing for functionality involves understanding user needs, defining features, and implementing them effectively to deliver value to the end-users.

Question 3: How does the design objective of performance impact software development?
Answer: Performance is essential because it determines how efficiently the software executes its functions. Meeting performance objectives involves optimizing algorithms, code, and resource utilization to ensure the software runs smoothly, responds quickly, and doesn't waste system resources.

Question 4: Explain the significance of usability as a design objective in software development.
Answer: Usability is vital because it focuses on the user experience. Designing for usability means creating intuitive, user-friendly interfaces and workflows, making it easier for users to interact with the software. Usable software improves user satisfaction and productivity.

Question 5: What does scalability mean as a design objective, and why is it important?
Answer: Scalability refers to the software's ability to handle increasing workloads or data volumes without a significant decrease in performance. It is crucial because it ensures the software remains effective as user demands grow, preventing bottlenecks and slowdowns as the system expands. Designing for scalability involves considering factors like architecture, databases, and load balancing.

7.2 Design Principles

Question 1: What is the "Single Responsibility Principle" in software design, and why is it important?
Answer: The Single Responsibility Principle states that a class should have only one reason to change. In other words, it should have a single, well-defined responsibility or job. This principle is essential because it promotes code modularity, making it easier to maintain and extend the software.

Question 2: Can you explain the "Open/Closed Principle" and its significance in software design?
Answer: The Open/Closed Principle suggests that software entities (classes, modules, functions) should be open for extension but closed for modification. This means you should be able to add new functionality without changing existing code. It is important because it encourages software to be more adaptable and less prone to introducing new bugs when extending its capabilities.

Question 3: What is "Liskov Substitution Principle" (LSP), and how does it affect software design?
Answer: The Liskov Substitution Principle states that objects of a derived class should be able to replace objects of the base class without affecting the correctness of the program. It enforces behavioral compatibility and helps ensure that subclasses do not break the behavior expected of the base class. It plays a crucial role in maintaining the integrity of the software's architecture.

Question 4: Explain the concept of "Interface Segregation Principle" in software design and its application.
Answer: The Interface Segregation Principle suggests that many small, specific interfaces are better than one large, general-purpose interface. This principle promotes design simplicity and avoids forcing classes to implement methods they don't need. It leads to more flexible and maintainable code.

Question 5: What is the "Dependency Inversion Principle," and why is it a fundamental design principle?

Answer: The Dependency Inversion Principle encourages high-level modules to depend on abstractions, not on low-level modules. It also emphasizes that both should depend on abstractions. This principle is crucial because it reduces coupling between modules, making the code more flexible and easier to maintain, test, and extend. It promotes the use of interfaces or abstract classes to decouple components.

7.3 Constructive Design Principles

Question 1: What are Constructive Design Principles, and how do they differ from other design principles?
Answer: Constructive Design Principles focus on how to build software systems by emphasizing the creation of clean and efficient designs. They differ from other design principles as they provide guidelines on how to proactively create well-structured and maintainable software rather than just identifying issues in existing designs.

Question 2: Can you explain the "Separation of Concerns" principle and its role in Constructive Design?
Answer: The Separation of Concerns principle advocates dividing a software system into distinct modules or components, each addressing a specific concern. This reduces complexity, enhances maintainability, and allows for easier updates. In Constructive Design, it's crucial for building systems that are modular and easy to extend.

Question 3: How does "High Cohesion" contribute to Constructive Design Principles?
Answer: High Cohesion is a constructive design principle that promotes designing modules or classes in a way that each has a single, well-defined purpose. This ensures that code is focused and does one thing exceptionally well, making it easier to maintain, test, and understand.

Question 4: What is "Low Coupling," and how does it enhance Constructive Design?
Answer: Low Coupling emphasizes minimizing dependencies between modules or components, allowing them to operate independently. In Constructive Design, low coupling is vital because it makes it easier to change or replace components without impacting the entire system, improving flexibility and maintainability.

Question 5: Explain the role of "Abstraction" in Constructive Design Principles.
Answer: Abstraction is a key Constructive Design Principle that involves creating simplified models of complex systems. By abstracting details, it makes it easier to design, understand, and communicate about software. Abstraction helps in achieving high-quality, clean, and understandable designs that are easier to implement and maintain.

7.4 Effective Modular Design

7.4.1 Functional Independence

Question 1: What does "Functional Independence" mean in software design, and why is it important?
Answer: Functional Independence refers to the concept of designing software components or modules that perform specific, well-defined functions without relying heavily on other parts of the system. It is important because it reduces interdependencies, making it easier to modify, maintain, and test individual components, leading to more robust and maintainable software.

Question 2: How does Functional Independence relate to modularity in software design?
Answer: Functional Independence is closely related to modularity. When modules or components are functionally independent, they can be treated as self-contained entities, promoting a modular design. This modularity enhances the reusability and maintainability of the software.

Question 3: Can you provide an example of a situation where Functional Independence has a significant impact on software design?
Answer: A classic example is the separation of user interface components from the core business logic in an application. By making the user interface components functionally independent of the business logic, changes to the user interface won't require modifications in the core logic. This separation simplifies design and maintenance.

Question 4: How does Functional Independence contribute to the testability of a software system?

Answer: Functional Independence makes it easier to test individual components in isolation. When components are self-contained and don't rely heavily on others, it simplifies unit testing, as you can focus on testing a specific function or feature without the complexity of the entire system.

Question 5: What are some potential challenges when trying to achieve Functional Independence in software design, and how can they be addressed?
Answer: Challenges may include identifying clear and well-defined boundaries between components, handling data flow between them, and avoiding excessive inter-component communication. These challenges can be addressed by following design principles such as the Single Responsibility Principle, Separation of Concerns, and Interface Segregation Principle. Proper documentation and communication within the development team are also important to ensure a clear understanding of component boundaries.

7.4.2 Cohesion and Coupling

Question 1: What is "Cohesion" in software design, and why is it important?
Answer: Cohesion refers to the degree to which the responsibilities of a software module or component are related and focused on a single, well-defined task. High cohesion is important because it leads to more maintainable, understandable, and reusable code by ensuring that each module has a clear, distinct purpose.

Question 2: Explain the different levels of cohesion in software design.
Answer: Cohesion can be categorized into several levels, including:
Functional Cohesion: When a module performs a single, specific function.
Sequential Cohesion: When a module performs multiple functions in a specific sequence.
Communicational Cohesion: When a module performs various functions related to a specific data structure.
Temporal Cohesion: When a module performs functions that need to be executed at the same time.
Procedural Cohesion: When a module groups functions that are called in a specific order.
Logical Cohesion: When a module groups functions that have a logical relationship.

Question 3: What is "Coupling" in software design, and how does it impact software quality?
Answer: Coupling refers to the degree of interdependence between software modules or components. High coupling increases the risk of side effects when making changes and can make the software less maintainable. It is crucial to keep coupling low to improve software quality and maintainability.

Question 4: Explain the types of coupling in software design.
Answer: There are several types of coupling, including:
Content Coupling: When one module accesses the internal data of another.
Common Coupling: When multiple modules share global data.
Control Coupling: When one module controls the flow or execution of another.
Stamp Coupling: When two modules share a composite data structure.
Data Coupling: When modules communicate by passing data, such as function parameters.
No Coupling (or Loose Coupling): When modules have no direct dependencies on each other.

Question 5: How can you improve Cohesion and reduce Coupling in software design?
Answer: To improve cohesion, focus on ensuring that each module has a single, clear responsibility. To reduce coupling, follow these practices:
Minimize the use of global variables or shared state.
Use well-defined interfaces and encapsulation.
Apply the Dependency Inversion Principle to decouple high-level and low-level modules.
Use design patterns like the Observer pattern to reduce direct dependencies.
Regularly review the software architecture to identify and reduce coupling where possible.

7.5 Design Heuristics for Effective Modularity

Question 1: What is the significance of modularity in software design?

Answer: Modularity is crucial in software design because it promotes the organization of complex systems into manageable, self-contained modules. It enhances reusability, maintainability, and understandability of code, making it easier to develop and adapt software systems.

Question 2: Can you explain the "High Cohesion" design heuristic and how it contributes to modularity?
Answer: High Cohesion means that modules or components should have a single, well-defined purpose or responsibility. This design heuristic contributes to modularity by ensuring that each module is focused on doing one thing exceptionally well, reducing interdependencies and simplifying the overall design.

Question 3: How does "Low Coupling" improve modularity in software systems?
Answer: Low Coupling encourages minimizing dependencies between modules or components. This design heuristic enhances modularity by reducing the impact of changes in one module on other parts of the system. It allows for more flexible, independent modules that are easier to maintain and replace.

Question 4: What role does "Information Hiding" play in achieving effective modularity?
Answer: Information Hiding, also known as encapsulation, involves restricting access to the internal details of a module. It contributes to effective modularity by allowing modules to hide their implementation details from other parts of the system. This reduces dependencies and ensures that changes to a module's internals do not affect the rest of the system.

Question 5: How can adherence to the "Single Responsibility Principle" improve modularity?
Answer: The Single Responsibility Principle suggests that a module should have a single, well-defined reason to change. Following this principle results in more modular software because each module has a clear and distinct responsibility. This makes it easier to understand, maintain, and extend the software while keeping modules self-contained.

7.6 Design Model

Question 1: What is a Design Model in software engineering, and how does it differ from a Requirements Model?
Answer: A Design Model is a representation of how a software system should be constructed. It describes the structure and organization of the system's components. Unlike a Requirements Model, which focuses on what the system should do, a Design Model focuses on how the system should do it.

Question 2: Can you explain the purpose of a Structural Design Model, and provide an example?
Answer: A Structural Design Model depicts the organization and relationships between the system's components. An example is the Class Diagram in UML, which shows classes, attributes, and associations. It helps developers understand the static structure of the system.

Question 3: What is a Behavioral Design Model, and how does it assist in software design?
Answer: A Behavioral Design Model describes how the system's components interact and function over time. Examples include Sequence Diagrams and State chart Diagrams in UML. Behavioral models help in understanding dynamic aspects, such as interactions and state transitions.

Question 4: How does the use of a Design Model aid in communication within a development team?
Answer: Design Models provide a visual and standardized way to represent the software system's structure and behavior. They facilitate communication by offering a common language for developers, architects, and stakeholders to discuss and understand the system's design, leading to more effective collaboration.

Question 5: What is the relationship between a Design Model and the actual software implementation, and how can it influence the development process?
Answer: A Design Model serves as a blueprint for the software system but is not the actual code. However, it significantly influences the development process. It helps in planning, guiding coding efforts, and ensuring that the implemented system aligns with the intended design. It also simplifies maintenance and updates by providing a clear reference for developers.

7.7 Design Implementation

Question 1: What is the role of Design Implementation in the software development process?
Answer: Design Implementation is the phase where the software design is translated into executable code. It involves writing, testing, and integrating the code components to create the actual software system. It bridges the gap between design and functioning software.

Question 2: How does Design Implementation contribute to the maintainability and scalability of a software system?
Answer: During Design Implementation, code is organized based on design principles, which enhances maintainability. Well-implemented designs make it easier to locate and fix bugs, add new features, and adapt to changing requirements. Additionally, a properly implemented design can provide a scalable foundation for future expansions.

Question 3: What role does code optimization play in Design Implementation, and why is it important?
Answer: Code optimization in Design Implementation involves enhancing code performance and efficiency. It is crucial because efficient code reduces resource consumption, improves system response times, and minimizes hardware requirements, leading to a better user experience and cost savings.

Question 4: How can version control and code repositories benefit Design Implementation?
Answer: Version control systems (e.g., Git) and code repositories (e.g., GitHub) help manage and track changes in code during implementation. They allow developers to collaborate, maintain a history of code modifications, and facilitate the easy recovery of previous code states. This ensures transparency, teamwork, and code integrity.

Question 5: What is the significance of testing and quality assurance during Design Implementation?
Answer: Testing and quality assurance are critical components of Design Implementation. They help identify and rectify issues and defects in the code, ensuring that the software behaves as intended. Quality assurance practices, such as code reviews and automated testing, enhance the reliability and stability of the final product.

Online Resources

Chapter 7 YouTube Playlist Link:
Link: https://www.youtube.com/playlist?list=PLzlh_31VWEFrAS1b7aFQ0Dr9K0uIH1tLY
QR Code:

Online Exam Paper Link:
Link: https://forms.gle/SBHmhtNdQzkgRHN79
QR Code:

MCQ Video Playlist Link:
Link: https://youtu.be/YQd6ArO6gL4
QR Code:

True/False Video Playlist Link:
Link: https://youtu.be/s8-3aHsq_SE
QR Code:

Online MCQ Exam Paper Link:
Link: https://forms.office.com/r/WW6M1MLi4W
QR Code:

Online True/False Exam Paper Link:
Link: https://forms.office.com/r/uQxtutrvup
QR Code:

Chapter 8: Design Concept

8.1 Design Concepts

Question 1: What is the significance of design concepts in software development?
Answer: Design concepts are fundamental principles and ideas that guide the creation of effective software solutions. They help ensure that software is well-structured, maintainable, and scalable. Understanding and applying design concepts is essential for producing high-quality software.

Question 2: Can you explain the difference between "Design Concepts" and "Design Patterns"?
Answer: Design Concepts are broad principles and ideas that provide guidelines for designing software. In contrast, Design Patterns are specific reusable solutions to common design problems. Design Concepts serve as the foundation for understanding and applying Design Patterns effectively.

Question 3: How do "Abstraction" and "Encapsulation" contribute to sound software design?
Answer: Abstraction involves simplifying complex systems by focusing on essential details while hiding irrelevant complexity. Encapsulation restricts access to the internal state of a module. These concepts enhance software design by making it more modular, understandable, and adaptable.

Question 4: What is the role of "Scalability" in software design, and why is it important?
Answer: Scalability refers to a system's ability to handle increased workloads or growth without sacrificing performance. It is crucial in software design because it ensures that the system can adapt to changing demands, making it a valuable asset in the long term.

Question 5: How can "Modularity" enhance software design, and what are its benefits?
Answer: Modularity involves dividing a system into separate, self-contained modules that interact through well-defined interfaces. Modularity improves software design by promoting code reusability, maintainability, and ease of collaboration among developers. It simplifies the process of extending or modifying the system without impacting the entire codebase.

8.1.1 Abstraction

Question 1: What is Abstraction in the context of software design?
Answer: Abstraction is the process of simplifying complex systems by identifying and focusing on essential details while ignoring irrelevant or low-level specifics. It involves creating a high-level representation of a concept or system to better understand, communicate, and work with it.

Question 2: How does Abstraction help in software design?
Answer: Abstraction in software design simplifies the development and understanding of systems by hiding unnecessary complexity. It allows designers and developers to work with a higher-level representation, making it easier to manage and maintain large software systems. Abstraction also supports the creation of reusable components and promotes efficient problem-solving.

Question 3: Can you provide an example of Abstraction in software design?
Answer: A common example of abstraction is the use of a programming language. When writing code, developers work with high-level constructs like functions and classes, abstracting away the underlying hardware-specific details. This allows developers to create software without needing to understand the low-level intricacies of the computer's architecture.

Question 4: What is the relationship between Abstraction and Encapsulation?
Answer: Abstraction and Encapsulation are related but distinct concepts. Abstraction involves simplifying complex systems by emphasizing essential details. Encapsulation, on the other hand, restricts access to the internal state of an object, making it a self-contained unit. While Abstraction focuses on what to show and what to hide, Encapsulation focuses on how to hide.

Question 5: How does Abstraction impact the maintainability and adaptability of software systems?
Answer: Abstraction enhances the maintainability and adaptability of software systems by reducing the complexity of the system. It isolates high-level functionality from implementation details, making it easier to modify or extend the software without affecting the entire codebase. Abstraction also makes it simpler to document and communicate the design and functionality of a system.

8.1.2 Refinement

Question 1: What is the concept of Refinement in software engineering?
Answer: Refinement is the process of gradually elaborating and expanding a high-level, abstract design or specification into more detailed and concrete representations. It involves breaking down complex systems into smaller, more manageable components and refining each of them in a step-by-step manner.

Question 2: Why is Refinement an important aspect of the software development process?
Answer: Refinement is essential because it enables a systematic approach to software development. It allows developers to work from abstract ideas to concrete implementations, reducing the risk of misunderstandings or errors and providing a clear path for turning design concepts into functional software.

Question 3: Can you explain the relationship between Refinement and the Waterfall Model of software development?
Answer: In the Waterfall Model, Refinement is a key component of each phase. Requirements are refined into detailed specifications, which are further refined into design, and so on. This sequential refinement process helps ensure that each stage of the project is well-prepared before moving to the next.

Question 4: What are some common techniques used for Refinement in software design?
Answer: Common refinement techniques include decomposition (breaking down complex systems into smaller components), stepwise refinement (gradually adding detail to high-level specifications), and data refinement (progressively defining data structures and their relationships).

Question 5: How does Refinement contribute to software maintainability and the ability to adapt to changing requirements?
Answer: By breaking down a system into manageable components and refining each component individually, Refinement simplifies maintenance and modifications. When requirements change, developers can update or replace specific components without affecting the entire system, making it more adaptable and cost-effective.

8.1.3 Modularity

Question 1: What is Modularity in software design, and why is it important?
Answer: Modularity is the practice of dividing a software system into separate, self-contained modules, each responsible for a specific function or feature. It is important because it promotes reusability, maintainability, and ease of collaboration among developers. By creating modular components, software systems become more flexible and less prone to errors.

Question 2: How can software developers achieve Modularity in their design and implementation?
Answer: Developers can achieve Modularity by breaking down a system into smaller, logically organized modules or components. These modules should have well-defined interfaces that specify how they interact with each other, making it easy to swap, update, or extend individual components without impacting the entire system.

Question 3: What is the relationship between Modularity and the Single Responsibility Principle?
Answer: Modularity aligns with the Single Responsibility Principle, which states that a module should have a single, well-defined reason to change. Both concepts encourage creating self-contained, focused modules, reducing complexity and enhancing maintainability.

Question 4: How does Modularity support code reusability and extensibility?

Answer: Modularity enables code reusability by allowing developers to use and adapt modules in different parts of a system or across projects. It also supports extensibility by making it easier to add new functionality without modifying existing code. This reduces the risk of introducing bugs and simplifies the development process.

Question 5: What are some common challenges and best practices when implementing Modularity in software systems?
Answer: Challenges can include defining clear module boundaries, managing inter-module dependencies, and avoiding excessive coupling. Best practices include using well-defined interfaces, employing design patterns, conducting code reviews, and adhering to principles such as the Separation of Concerns to ensure effective Modularity.

8.1.4 Software Architecture

Question 1: What is Software Architecture, and why is it a critical aspect of software development?
Answer: Software Architecture is the high-level structure of a software system that defines how its components and modules interact. It serves as a blueprint for the software's organization and behavior. It's essential because it guides the design process, ensures system reliability, scalability, and maintainability, and facilitates communication among development teams and stakeholders.

Question 2: How does Software Architecture differ from design patterns and coding practices?
Answer: Software Architecture focuses on the overall structure and organization of a system, defining how its components interact. In contrast, design patterns and coding practices are more specific and relate to solving particular design or coding problems within the architecture. While design patterns are solutions to recurring design issues, coding practices govern how code is written and formatted.

Question 3: What are some common architectural styles and patterns used in software design?
Answer: Common architectural styles include layered architecture, client-server architecture, and microservices architecture. Design patterns like the Model-View-Controller (MVC) and Singleton pattern are frequently used to address specific design challenges.

Question 4: How does a well-designed Software Architecture contribute to a software project's success?
Answer: A well-designed Software Architecture ensures that the system aligns with the project's goals and requirements. It promotes scalability, maintainability, and flexibility, which are essential for accommodating evolving needs and reducing technical debt. A robust architecture also enhances communication, making it easier to manage complexity and deliver a reliable software product.

Question 5: What role does Software Architecture play in bridging the gap between business requirements and technical solutions?
Answer: Software Architecture serves as a bridge between business requirements and technical solutions by translating high-level goals into a structured, actionable plan. It helps stakeholders visualize how the system will meet their needs and provides a framework for technical teams to implement and deliver those requirements effectively.

8.1.5 Control Hierarchy

Question 1: What is Control Hierarchy in the context of software design?
Answer: Control Hierarchy refers to the arrangement of control structures, such as loops and conditional statements, in a software system. It determines the order in which program instructions are executed and how decisions and iterations are controlled.

Question 2: Why is Control Hierarchy essential for software design and development?
Answer: Control Hierarchy is fundamental because it defines the flow of a program's logic, ensuring that instructions are executed in a specific order. A well-structured control hierarchy leads to software that is logical, readable, and performs its functions as intended.

Question 3: What are some common control structures used in control hierarchy?

Answer: Common control structures include if statements, switch statements, while loops, for loops, and do-while loops. These structures are used to control the flow of a program's execution based on conditions and iterations.

Question 4: How can a well-designed control hierarchy contribute to code readability and maintainability?
Answer: A well-designed control hierarchy follows clear and consistent patterns, making the code easier to read and understand. It simplifies the process of locating and fixing bugs or adding new features, enhancing code maintainability.

8.1.6 Structural Partitioning

Question 1: What is Structural Partitioning in software architecture?
Answer: Structural Partitioning is a design technique that involves dividing a complex software system into smaller, self-contained components or modules, each responsible for a specific aspect of the system's functionality. This division simplifies development, maintenance, and collaboration by isolating different concerns in the system.

Question 2: How does Structural Partitioning enhance the scalability of software systems?
Answer: Structural Partitioning contributes to scalability by creating a modular and extensible system. When you need to accommodate increased demands, you can scale individual modules or components independently, making it easier to expand specific areas of the system without affecting the entire application.

Question 3: Can you provide an example of how Structural Partitioning can improve software maintainability?
Answer: Consider an e-commerce platform that uses Structural Partitioning to separate its user management, order processing, and payment processing components. When a change is needed, developers can focus on the specific module without disrupting the functionality of the entire system, leading to easier maintenance and updates.

Question 4: What are some challenges that developers may face when implementing Structural Partitioning?
Answer: Challenges include defining clear module boundaries, managing inter-module dependencies, and ensuring consistent communication between modules. Addressing these challenges often requires well-defined interfaces, clear documentation, and rigorous design principles.

Question 5: How does Structural Partitioning support effective collaboration among development teams?
Answer: Structural Partitioning facilitates collaboration by breaking down a complex system into manageable components, allowing different teams or developers to work on specific modules independently. It ensures that each team can focus on their area of expertise, leading to more efficient development and improved teamwork.

8.2 Major Outlines of Design Specifications

Question 1: What are the major components of a Design Specification document?
Answer: A typical Design Specification document includes key components like system architecture, data structures, algorithms, user interfaces, modules, and their interactions. It also provides details on design constraints, error handling, and performance requirements.

Question 2: How does the system architecture section of a Design Specification document contribute to the development process?
Answer: The system architecture section defines the overall structure and organization of the software, including components, modules, and their interactions. It guides developers in implementing the system and ensures that it aligns with the project's goals and requirements.

Question 3: What is the significance of documenting data structures and algorithms in a Design Specification?
Answer: Documenting data structures and algorithms helps developers understand how the system processes and manipulates data. It ensures that the chosen data structures and algorithms are efficient, promoting optimal system performance.

Question 4: How do design constraints and error handling details affect the development of a software system?

Answer: Design constraints provide a set of rules and limitations that guide development, ensuring that the software complies with relevant standards and requirements. Error handling details define how the system responds to unexpected situations, enhancing reliability and user experience.

Question 5: Why is it important to include performance requirements in a Design Specification document?
Answer: Performance requirements outline the expected system performance, such as response times and throughput. They serve as benchmarks for assessing and optimizing the system's performance during development, helping to meet user expectations and business needs.

Online Resources

Chapter 8 YouTube Playlist Link:
Link: https://www.youtube.com/playlist?list=PLzlh_31VWEFo_-YP3k45xd9fLCxZuO6zf
QR Code:

Online Exam Paper Link:
Link: https://forms.gle/qfPcnJbnKsmkHEBm8
QR Code:

MCQ Video Playlist Link:
Link: https://youtu.be/L0cuwAtjXL0
QR Code:

True/False Video Playlist Link:
Link: https://youtu.be/e5xJ-vQxIR0
QR Code:

Online MCQ Exam Paper Link:
Link: https://forms.office.com/r/7s5C5F1x6G
QR Code:

Online True/False Exam Paper Link:
Link: https://forms.office.com/r/Ds7K1HcN3P
QR Code:

Chapter 9: Software Project Management (SPM)

9.1 Introduction Software Project Management (SPM)

Question 1: What is Software Project Management, and why is it crucial in software development?
Answer: Software Project Management is the discipline of planning, organizing, and overseeing software development projects from initiation to completion. It's crucial because it ensures that projects are delivered on time, within budget, and with the desired quality, meeting the needs of clients and stakeholders.

Question 2: How does Software Project Management differ from general project management?
Answer: Software Project Management focuses on the unique challenges and complexities of software development, such as the need for iterative and incremental processes, changing requirements, and technology advancements. It adapts project management principles to suit the specific demands of the software industry.

Question 3: What are the key responsibilities of a Software Project Manager?
Answer: A Software Project Manager is responsible for project planning, resource allocation, risk management, scope control, and ensuring that the project is on track to meet its objectives. They also facilitate communication among team members, stakeholders, and clients.

Question 4: How can effective Software Project Management contribute to the success of a project?
Answer: Effective Software Project Management helps ensure that projects are completed on time, within budget, and with high-quality outcomes. It minimizes risks, enhances team collaboration, and allows for better control and monitoring of project progress, ultimately increasing the likelihood of project success.

Question 5: What are some common challenges in Software Project Management, and how can they be addressed?
Answer: Common challenges include changing requirements, scope creep, resource constraints, and managing risks. These challenges can be addressed through thorough planning, regular communication with stakeholders, implementing agile methodologies, and using project management tools and techniques to track progress and adapt to changes.

9.2 Project Management Process

Question 1: What is the Project Management Process, and why is it essential in project management?
Answer: The Project Management Process is a series of phases and activities that guide a project from initiation to completion. It's essential because it provides a structured framework for planning, executing, and monitoring projects, ensuring they are delivered on time, within budget, and with the desired quality.

Question 2: Can you explain the key phases of the Project Management Process?
Answer: The Project Management Process typically includes phases such as initiation, planning, execution, monitoring and control, and closure. During initiation, the project's objectives and feasibility are assessed. Planning involves defining project scope, creating schedules, and allocating resources. Execution is the actual work phase, followed by monitoring and control to ensure the project stays on track. Closure marks the project's completion and includes activities like final testing and project handover.

Question 3: How does effective Project Management Process contribute to project success?
Answer: Effective Project Management Process provides structure and clarity, reduces uncertainty, and enhances communication. It ensures that projects are well-organized and adhere to timelines and budgets, leading to successful project delivery.

Question 4: What role does risk management play in the Project Management Process?
Answer: Risk management is an integral part of the Project Management Process. It involves identifying potential risks, assessing their impact, and developing strategies to mitigate or respond to them. This proactive approach helps ensure that unexpected issues don't derail the project.

Question 5: How can Project Management Tools and Software support the Project Management Process?
Answer: Project Management Tools and Software automate tasks, facilitate communication, and provide real-time tracking and reporting. They help project managers and teams stay organized, collaborate effectively, and make data-driven decisions, ultimately improving the efficiency and success of the Project Management Process.

9.3 Project size estimation techniques

Question 1: What are Project Size Estimation Techniques, and why are they important in project management?
Answer: Project Size Estimation Techniques are methods used to assess the size of a software project, such as the volume of code, number of features, or user requirements. They are crucial because accurate size estimates help in planning resources, budget, and scheduling, which are essential for successful project management.

Question 2: Can you explain the difference between Function Point Analysis (FPA) and Lines of Code (LOC) as size estimation techniques?
Answer: Function Point Analysis (FPA) measures the functionality provided by a software system from a user's perspective, considering inputs, outputs, inquiries, files, and interfaces. In contrast, Lines of Code (LOC) simply measures the lines of code written. FPA provides a more user-centric view, while LOC offers a developer-centric view of project size.

Question 3: What are some common Project Size Estimation Techniques, and when are they typically used?
Answer: Common Project Size Estimation Techniques include Function Point Analysis (FPA), Use Case Points (UCP), Story Points, and Lines of Code (LOC). They are used at different stages of a project to assess size based on varying criteria, such as user requirements, features, or code volume.

Question 4: How do you choose the most appropriate Project Size Estimation Technique for a specific project?
Answer: The choice of a Project Size Estimation Technique depends on the project's nature, available data, and the level of accuracy required. For instance, FPA is ideal for user-centric projects, while LOC is suitable for code-centric projects. It's essential to consider the project's goals and constraints when selecting an estimation technique.

Question 5: What are the advantages of using Project Size Estimation Techniques in project management?
Answer: Project Size Estimation Techniques provide more accurate project size assessments, leading to better resource allocation, cost estimation, and scheduling. They enhance project planning and control, making it easier to manage and deliver projects successfully.

9.4 System configuration Management

Question 1: What is System Configuration Management, and why is it essential in software development?
Answer: System Configuration Management is the practice of managing and controlling the configuration items in a software system, including hardware, software, and documentation. It is essential because it ensures that all components are well-organized, versioned, and traceable throughout the development life cycle, facilitating efficient development, maintenance, and troubleshooting.

Question 2: Can you explain the key activities involved in System Configuration Management?
Answer: The key activities include configuration identification (defining and naming configuration items), configuration control (managing changes to items), configuration status accounting (tracking and reporting item status), and configuration auditing (ensuring compliance with standards and requirements).

Question 3: What role does version control play in System Configuration Management?
Answer: Version control is a critical aspect of System Configuration Management. It enables tracking changes made to software components over time, ensuring that different versions are properly documented, retrievable, and consistent. This prevents errors, facilitates collaboration, and supports rollbacks when issues arise.

Question 4: How does System Configuration Management enhance software quality and traceability?
Answer: System Configuration Management helps maintain the integrity and consistency of software components, reducing the risk of errors and inconsistencies. It also provides traceability, allowing for the documentation of changes and a clear audit trail, which is invaluable for quality control and compliance.

Question 5: What are some common tools and practices used in System Configuration Management?
Answer: Common tools include version control systems like Git, issue tracking software, and configuration management databases (CMDBs). Practices involve defining configuration baselines, implementing change control processes, and conducting regular audits to ensure the system's integrity.

9.5 Capability maturity model (CMM)

Question 1: What is the significance of Size Estimation and Cost Estimation in software project management?
Answer: Size Estimation and Cost Estimation are essential processes for understanding the scope of a software project. Size Estimation quantifies the size of the software product, while Cost Estimation determines the financial resources needed for development. Accurate estimations are critical for planning, budgeting, and resource allocation.

Question 2: Can you explain the difference between Function Points and Lines of Code as Size Estimation metrics?
Answer: Function Points measure the functionality provided by software from a user's perspective, while Lines of Code (LOC) quantify the actual lines of code written. Function Points offer a more user-centric view of size, while LOC provides a developer-centric view.

Question 3: How does a well-executed Size Estimation process impact the Cost Estimation and project planning?
Answer: A well-executed Size Estimation process provides the foundation for accurate Cost Estimation. It enables project managers to calculate resource requirements, budget constraints, and project timelines more precisely. This information helps in effective project planning and ensures that resources are allocated efficiently.

Question 4: What are the common challenges in Size Estimation and Cost Estimation, and how can they be addressed?
Answer: Challenges include evolving requirements, limited historical data, and changing technology. To address these challenges, software project managers should continuously update and validate their estimation models, track actual versus estimated costs, and use agile development practices to adapt to changing requirements.

Question 5: How do risk factors, such as project complexity and technology constraints, impact Size and Cost Estimations?
Answer: Risk factors can significantly affect Size and Cost Estimations. Projects with higher complexity or unfamiliar technology may have increased uncertainty and risk. It's important to account for these factors in the estimation process, by providing contingency reserves and conducting sensitivity analysis to better handle potential risks.

9.6 Size Estimation and Cost Estimation

9.6.1 Methods of Size Estimation (LOC, FP, etc.)

Question 1: What are the key methods used for Size Estimation in software project management, and when are they typically applied?
Answer: Common methods include Lines of Code (LOC), Function Points (FP), and Story Points. LOC is used to estimate project size based on the lines of code written. FP focuses on functionality from a user's perspective, while Story Points are used in agile methodologies to estimate the complexity of user stories.

Question 2: How does Lines of Code (LOC) differ from Function Points (FP) as Size Estimation metrics?
Answer: Lines of Code (LOC) quantifies the actual lines of code written, providing a developer-centric view of size. Function Points (FP) measure the functionality from a user's perspective, offering a more user-centric view of the size, independent of coding style or language.

Question 3: In what situations is the Function Point (FP) method more suitable for Size Estimation than Lines of Code (LOC)?

Answer: Function Points (FP) are more suitable when estimating size for projects where the focus is on user functionality, independent of the underlying technology or coding language. FP is particularly useful for measuring the user's view of the software, making it a valuable metric for assessing software systems with diverse architectures and technologies.

Question 4: How do Story Points contribute to Size Estimation, and when are they commonly used?
Answer: Story Points are commonly used in agile software development to estimate the effort or complexity of user stories or features. They provide a relative measure of work, allowing teams to estimate the size and effort required for backlog items. Story Points are particularly useful in iterative and incremental development approaches.

Question 5: What are the advantages and limitations of using different Size Estimation methods, and how can they impact project planning?
Answer: The advantages of different methods vary depending on the project's characteristics. LOC provides a precise view of code volume, but it may not reflect functionality accurately. FP and Story Points offer a more user-centric perspective but can be more complex to calculate. Choosing the right method depends on project goals and the need for accurate planning and resource allocation.

9.6.2 Cost Estimation Models

Question 1: What are Cost Estimation Models, and why are they essential in software project management?
Answer: Cost Estimation Models are mathematical algorithms or methods used to predict the financial resources required for a software project. They are essential because they provide a systematic and data-driven approach to budgeting and resource allocation, helping organizations plan and manage their projects effectively.

Question 2: Can you explain the difference between the Basic COCOMO model and the Intermediate COCOMO model in software cost estimation?
Answer: The Basic COCOMO model estimates project costs based on size, complexity, and development mode. The Intermediate COCOMO model, in addition to these factors, considers various cost drivers, offering a more comprehensive and accurate estimation.

Question 3: What is the role of parametric models like SEER-SEM and the Putnam Model in software cost estimation?
Answer: Parametric models like SEER-SEM and the Putnam Model use historical data and parametric equations to estimate project costs. They are useful for organizations with access to substantial historical project data and provide a data-centric approach to cost estimation.

Question 4: How do expert judgment and analogy-based estimation contribute to cost estimation?
Answer: Expert judgment involves experienced professionals using their knowledge to make informed estimates. Analogy-based estimation leverages similarities with past projects to estimate costs. Both methods provide valuable insights when historical data is limited, and expert input is required.

Question 5: What are some common challenges in cost estimation, and how can organizations address them?
Answer: Challenges include evolving requirements, uncertainty, and changing technology. Organizations can address these challenges by continually updating and validating their cost estimation models, using sensitivity analysis to account for uncertainties, and adopting agile practices to adapt to changing project requirements.

9.6.3 COCOMO Model (Introduction)

Question 1: What is the COCOMO (Constructive Cost Model), and what is its primary purpose in software engineering?
Answer: COCOMO is a widely used software cost estimation model developed by Dr. Barry Boehm. Its primary purpose is to estimate the effort, cost, and duration of a software project based on various project characteristics and parameters.

Question 2: Can you explain the key components of the COCOMO model?

Answer: The COCOMO model consists of three levels: Basic COCOMO, Intermediate COCOMO, and Detailed COCOMO. Basic COCOMO estimates cost based on project size and development mode. Intermediate COCOMO adds cost drivers, while Detailed COCOMO provides a more comprehensive estimation by considering various factors in detail.

Question 3: What is the difference between the Organic, Semi-Detached, and Embedded development modes in COCOMO?
Answer: These development modes in COCOMO reflect the complexity of software projects. Organic mode is for simple, well-understood projects. Semi-Detached is for moderately complex projects, while Embedded is for highly complex, critical projects with extensive technical requirements.

Question 4: How does COCOMO handle cost drivers, and why are they significant in cost estimation?
Answer: COCOMO introduces cost drivers to account for various project-specific factors, such as team experience, software tools, and product characteristics. Cost drivers significantly influence the estimation accuracy, as they adjust the project cost based on these specific attributes.

Question 5: What are some best practices for effectively using COCOMO in software project management?
Answer: To use COCOMO effectively, it's essential to have a clear understanding of the project's characteristics, gather accurate data, and regularly update the estimation as the project progresses. It's also important to use COCOMO in conjunction with other estimation methods and to involve experienced professionals for the most accurate results.

9.6.4 Estimating Risks and Contingencies

Question 1: What is the importance of estimating risks and contingencies in project management?
Answer: Estimating risks and contingencies is crucial for identifying potential project threats and planning for unforeseen events. It allows project managers to proactively manage risks, ensuring that projects stay on track, within budget, and meet objectives.

Question 2: How do you typically identify and assess risks in a project?
Answer: Risks can be identified through brainstorming, historical data, expert judgment, and risk registers. They are assessed by considering their impact, likelihood, and timing, which helps prioritize risks and determine appropriate responses.

Question 3: What is the difference between qualitative and quantitative risk analysis, and when should each be used?
Answer: Qualitative risk analysis involves assessing risks based on subjective judgment and categorizing them by severity. Quantitative risk analysis, on the other hand, assigns numerical values to risks, allowing for more precise modeling and prioritization. Qualitative analysis is typically used in the early stages of risk identification, while quantitative analysis is employed when more detailed and numeric data is available.

Question 4: How do you determine contingency reserves based on risk estimates?
Answer: Contingency reserves are typically calculated as a percentage of the project budget or schedule. The percentage can vary based on the project's risk exposure. Higher-risk projects may require larger contingency reserves to cover potential risk-related costs.

Question 5: Can you provide an example of a risk response strategy and how it is implemented in a project?
Answer: One common risk response strategy is "mitigation," which involves taking proactive actions to reduce the likelihood or impact of a risk. For instance, if the risk is that a key team member may leave the project, a mitigation strategy could involve cross-training team members to ensure that others can step in if needed. Mitigation strategies are implemented as part of the project plan and are continually monitored for effectiveness.

9.7 Software Project Planning

Question 1: What is Software Project Planning, and why is it a critical phase in project management?

Answer: Software Project Planning is the process of defining project objectives, scope, timelines, resource allocation, and risk management. It's a critical phase because it lays the groundwork for successful project execution, helping to ensure that projects are completed on time, within budget, and with high quality.

Question 2: How do you initiate the Software Project Planning process, and what are its primary components?
Answer: Initiating the process involves understanding the project's goals, identifying stakeholders, defining scope, and assessing project feasibility. The primary components include project objectives, schedules, resource allocation, budgets, risk assessment, and communication plans.

Question 3: What role do project constraints, such as scope, time, and budget, play in Software Project Planning?
Answer: Project constraints, often referred to as the "triple constraint," are central to project planning. They define the boundaries and limitations of the project. Effective planning ensures that the project stays within these constraints while delivering the expected results.

Question 4: How can Agile methodologies be integrated into Software Project Planning, and what are the benefits of this approach?
Answer: Agile methodologies promote flexibility and adaptability in project planning. They allow for iterative planning and frequent reassessment of project goals, enabling teams to respond to changing requirements. The benefits include improved responsiveness to customer needs and a higher likelihood of delivering a valuable product.

Question 5: Can you provide an example of a situation where effective Software Project Planning led to a successful project outcome?
Answer: In a situation where project planning was executed effectively, the team defined clear project objectives, accurately estimated resources, and assessed potential risks. The project was delivered on time, within budget, and met all the set objectives, resulting in high customer satisfaction and business success.

9.7.1 Project Initiation

Question 1: What is Project Initiation, and why is it a crucial phase in project management?
Answer: Project Initiation is the first phase in the project management process, where the project's objectives, scope, feasibility, and stakeholders are defined. It's crucial because it sets the project's foundation, aligns it with organizational goals, and ensures that it's worth pursuing.

Question 2: How do you determine if a project is feasible during the initiation phase, and what factors are typically assessed?
Answer: Feasibility is assessed by evaluating factors like technical, financial, operational, and scheduling aspects. This phase considers the project's technical complexity, resource availability, cost estimates, and the alignment with organizational strategy.

Question 3: What role do stakeholders play in project initiation, and how do you identify and engage them effectively?
Answer: Stakeholders are individuals or groups who have a vested interest in the project. Identifying and engaging them effectively involves techniques such as stakeholder analysis, surveys, and meetings to understand their needs, expectations, and concerns. Engaging stakeholders from the beginning helps ensure their support throughout the project.

Question 4: Can you explain the process of defining project objectives during project initiation?
Answer: Defining project objectives involves identifying the project's purpose, goals, and expected outcomes. Objectives should be SMART (Specific, Measurable, Achievable, Relevant, and Time-bound) and aligned with the organization's strategic goals.

Question 5: How does a well-executed project initiation phase impact the overall project's success?
Answer: A well-executed project initiation phase leads to a clear understanding of project objectives, realistic planning, and alignment with stakeholder expectations. This, in turn, reduces the risk of scope changes, budget overruns, and project delays, significantly enhancing the likelihood of a successful project outcome.

9.7.2 Planning Scope Management

Question 1: What is Planning Scope Management, and why is it a critical part of project planning?
Answer: Planning Scope Management is the process of defining, documenting, and managing project scope. It's critical because it ensures a clear understanding of what's included and excluded from the project, which is essential for project success and preventing scope creep.

Question 2: Can you explain the difference between product scope and project scope in the context of scope management?
Answer: Product scope refers to the features and functionalities of the project's deliverables, while project scope defines the work required to produce those deliverables. Product scope relates to what the product will do, while project scope defines how it will be done.

Question 3: How do you collect requirements and create a Work Breakdown Structure (WBS) during scope management?
Answer: Collecting requirements involves interviewing stakeholders, reviewing documents, and using tools like surveys to identify project needs. Creating a Work Breakdown Structure (WBS) involves decomposing the project into smaller, manageable tasks, which helps in clearly defining the scope and planning project work.

Question 4: What are the common challenges in scope management, and how can they be addressed?
Answer: Common challenges include scope changes, uncontrolled scope creep, and inadequate stakeholder involvement. These issues can be addressed through effective change control processes, regular communication with stakeholders, and detailed scope documentation and planning.

Question 5: How does effective scope management impact project outcomes, such as budget, schedule, and quality?
Answer: Effective scope management ensures that the project stays within the defined boundaries, which prevents budget overruns and schedule delays. It also contributes to higher quality outcomes by ensuring that project requirements are well-defined and met. Proper scope management is a key driver of project success.

9.7.3 Work Breakdown Structure (WBS)

Question 1: What is a Work Breakdown Structure (WBS), and how does it contribute to project management?
Answer: A Work Breakdown Structure (WBS) is a hierarchical decomposition of a project into smaller, manageable work packages or tasks. It helps in organizing, defining, and visualizing the scope of a project, making it easier to plan, track, and manage project work.

Question 2: Can you explain the key components of a WBS, such as the top-level node, work packages, and control accounts?
Answer: A WBS typically includes a top-level node representing the entire project, which is further broken down into major deliverables or control accounts. Control accounts are then divided into work packages, which are the smallest units of work. Work packages are detailed enough to be assigned, estimated, and tracked.

Question 3: How do you create a WBS, and what techniques can be used to decompose project work effectively?
Answer: Creating a WBS involves collaborating with stakeholders to define project scope and objectives. Effective decomposition can be achieved through techniques such as brainstorming, mind mapping, expert judgment, and using historical data or templates from previous projects.

Question 4: What are the advantages of using a WBS in project management, and how does it facilitate project planning and control?
Answer: A WBS provides clarity, structure, and a common understanding of the project scope. It aids in better resource allocation, task assignment, and project scheduling. It also helps in monitoring progress, controlling scope, and managing project risks.

Question 5: Can you provide an example of a situation where a well-constructed WBS significantly improved project management and outcomes?
Answer: In a complex construction project, a well-constructed WBS enabled the project manager to efficiently allocate resources, track progress, and manage costs. The detailed breakdown allowed for better control of project elements, resulting in timely completion, cost savings, and high-quality deliverables.

9.7.4 Creating a Project Schedule

Question 1: What is the importance of creating a project schedule, and how does it contribute to successful project management?
Answer: Creating a project schedule is essential for defining the timeline, sequencing tasks, and allocating resources. It ensures that the project stays on track, meets deadlines, and enables efficient resource management, ultimately contributing to the project's successful completion.

Question 2: Can you explain the key components of a project schedule, such as tasks, dependencies, milestones, and critical path?
Answer: A project schedule includes a list of tasks, their durations, dependencies (relationships between tasks), milestones (significant events), and the critical path (the longest path through the project network, which determines the project's duration).

Question 3: How do you determine task durations and dependencies when creating a project schedule?
Answer: Task durations can be estimated based on historical data, expert judgment, or using techniques like PERT analysis. Task dependencies are determined by identifying which tasks are reliant on others, creating a logical sequence for project work.

Question 4: What role does resource allocation and leveling play in creating a project schedule?
Answer: Resource allocation involves assigning resources (e.g., people, equipment) to specific tasks. Resource leveling is the process of adjusting resource assignments to avoid overallocating or underallocating resources, ensuring a balanced workload throughout the project.

Question 5: Can you provide an example of a situation where a well-constructed project schedule was crucial in managing a project effectively?
Answer: In a software development project, a well-constructed project schedule helped the team manage various tasks, including coding, testing, and documentation. By defining dependencies and critical paths, the team could efficiently allocate resources, avoid bottlenecks, and meet tight project deadlines, resulting in a successful software release.

9.7.5 Risk Identification and Management

Question 1: What is Risk Identification and Management, and why is it a critical aspect of project planning?
Answer: Risk Identification and Management involves identifying potential threats and opportunities, assessing their impact and likelihood, and developing strategies to mitigate or leverage them. It's critical because it helps project managers proactively address uncertainties, avoid problems, and maximize project success.

Question 2: How do you identify and categorize risks during the risk identification process?
Answer: Risk identification involves brainstorming, reviewing historical data, consulting experts, and using checklists. Risks can be categorized as internal (within the project) and external (outside the project), as well as positive (opportunities) and negative (threats).

Question 3: What are some common techniques for assessing and prioritizing risks in project management?
Answer: Techniques include qualitative assessment, where risks are ranked by impact and likelihood, and quantitative assessment, which assigns numerical values to risks. Risk matrices, risk registers, and Monte Carlo simulations are also useful for prioritizing risks.

Question 4: How do you develop and implement risk response strategies, and what is the role of contingency planning?
Answer: Developing risk response strategies involves choosing appropriate actions for each identified risk, which may include mitigation, avoidance, transfer, or acceptance. Contingency planning involves preparing for potential risks by setting aside resources, time, or budget as reserves.

Question 5: Can you provide an example of a situation where effective risk identification and management positively impacted a project's outcome?
Answer: In a construction project, the team's thorough risk identification and management process helped them identify the risk of unfavorable weather conditions. As a response strategy, they developed a contingency plan that included scheduling flexibility. When inclement weather occurred, the project was able to adjust without significant delays, ensuring the project was completed on time and within budget.

9.7.6 RMMM (Risk Mitigation, Monitoring, and Management)

Question 1: What is the purpose of the RMMM (Risk Mitigation, Monitoring, and Management) plan, and why is it an essential part of project risk management?
Answer: The RMMM plan outlines strategies for mitigating, monitoring, and managing project risks. It is essential because it provides a structured approach to identify, assess, and address risks throughout the project lifecycle, ensuring that risks do not disrupt project progress.

Question 2: How do you identify and assess risks as part of the RMMM process, and what criteria are used to prioritize risks?
Answer: Risk identification involves techniques like brainstorming and checklists, while risk assessment includes evaluating each risk's potential impact and likelihood. Risks are prioritized based on their severity, considering both the impact on project objectives and the probability of occurrence.

Question 3: Can you explain the key components of a comprehensive RMMM plan, including risk mitigation, risk monitoring, and risk management strategies?
Answer: A comprehensive RMMM plan includes risk identification, risk analysis, risk response strategies, risk monitoring and reporting procedures, and clear roles and responsibilities for risk management. Mitigation strategies outline actions to reduce risk impact, monitoring involves tracking identified risks, and management outlines responses to handle risks if they materialize.

Question 4: How does the RMMM plan contribute to project success, and how can it help project managers make informed decisions?
Answer: The RMMM plan enhances project success by proactively addressing risks, reducing the likelihood of disruptions, and minimizing the impact of unforeseen events. It provides project managers with a structured approach to risk management, helping them make informed decisions and adapt to changing project conditions.

Question 5: Can you provide an example of a situation where a well-executed RMMM plan positively impacted a project's outcome?
Answer: In a software development project, a comprehensive RMMM plan identified the risk of key team members leaving during the project. The plan included mitigation strategies such as knowledge transfer and cross-training. When one team member unexpectedly left, the project continued smoothly, thanks to these prepared responses, ensuring successful project completion.

9.8 Component-Based Engineering process

Question 1: What is Component-Based Engineering (CBE), and how does it differ from traditional software development?
Answer: Component-Based Engineering is an approach to software development that emphasizes the reuse of pre-built components. It differs from traditional development by focusing on assembling existing components to create applications rather than building everything from scratch, resulting in faster development and reduced costs.

Question 2: How do you select and integrate components into a CBE project, and what criteria do you consider for component compatibility?
Answer: Component selection involves identifying suitable components from libraries or repositories, considering factors like functionality, quality, and licensing. Integrating components requires understanding their interfaces and ensuring compatibility with the project's requirements and existing components.

Question 3: What are the advantages of using a CBE approach, and what challenges may arise during the process?
Answer: Advantages include faster development, reduced development costs, and improved software quality through the use of well-tested components. Challenges may include finding the right components, ensuring compatibility, and managing component dependencies.

Question 4: How does CBE impact software maintenance and scalability, and what strategies can be employed to address these aspects?
Answer: CBE simplifies maintenance by making it easier to update or replace components without affecting the entire system. To address scalability, organizations can plan for extensibility by designing systems with modular, pluggable components that can be scaled up or down as needed.

Question 5: Can you provide an example of a situation where the Component-Based Engineering process was successfully employed to develop a software application?
Answer: In a project involving e-commerce software development, a CBE approach allowed the team to quickly incorporate payment processing, shopping cart, and user authentication components from existing libraries. This accelerated development, reduced costs, and resulted in a robust e-commerce platform that met customer needs and could be easily maintained and extended.

Online Resources

Chapter 9 YouTube Playlist Link:
Link: https://www.youtube.com/playlist?list=PLzlh_31VWEFrHzSFXM2p559CFr2Bxk8WC
QR Code:

Online Exam Paper Link:
Link: https://forms.gle/ja8PvfRjgGAGUsCf8
QR Code:

MCQ Video Playlist Link:
Link: https://youtu.be/gZm4wPjo1uw
QR Code:

True/False Video Playlist Link:
Link: https://youtu.be/Ws2uqm37m6Y
QR Code:

Online MCQ Exam Paper Link:
Link: https://forms.office.com/r/B0b5PeRtBH
QR Code:

Online True/False Exam Paper Link:
Link: https://forms.office.com/r/h41EVRrmTu
QR Code:

Chapter 10: Software Testing, Debugging and Maintenance

10.1 Testing Objectives

Question 1: What are the primary objectives of software testing, and why is it a crucial phase in the software development process?
Answer: The primary objectives of software testing are to identify defects, ensure that the software meets quality standards, and verify that it functions correctly. Testing is critical because it helps in improving software quality, enhancing reliability, and minimizing the risk of software failures.

Question 2: Can you explain the difference between functional testing and non-functional testing, and why both are essential in achieving testing objectives?
Answer: Functional testing evaluates whether the software functions as intended, focusing on its features and capabilities. Non-functional testing assesses qualities like performance, security, and usability. Both are essential because they ensure the software not only works correctly but also meets user expectations and performs well under various conditions.

Question 3: How do you set specific testing objectives for a software testing project, and what factors influence these objectives?
Answer: Testing objectives are determined based on project goals, user requirements, and the software's intended use. Factors influencing testing objectives include the application's complexity, industry standards, and regulatory compliance requirements.

Question 4: What is the relationship between testing objectives and test cases, and how are test cases designed to meet specific objectives?
Answer: Test cases are designed to validate that specific functionality or non-functional aspects of the software meet the defined objectives. Each test case is created to target particular requirements or qualities, ensuring that the software performs as intended.

Question 5: Can you provide an example of a situation where clear testing objectives were instrumental in successfully delivering a high-quality software product?
Answer: In a healthcare software project, well-defined testing objectives ensured that the software met critical regulatory requirements for data security and privacy. By setting clear objectives and conducting rigorous testing to meet them, the project team was able to launch a secure and compliant software solution that enhanced patient trust and met industry standards.

10.2 Types of Software Testing

Question 1: What are the different types of software testing, and why is it essential to employ various testing types in the software development lifecycle?
Answer: Software testing includes various types like unit testing, integration testing, system testing, and user acceptance testing. It's important to use a combination of testing types because each type focuses on different aspects of the software, ensuring comprehensive evaluation and quality assurance.

Question 2: Can you explain the key differences between manual and automated testing, and when is each type typically used?
Answer: Manual testing involves human testers executing test cases, while automated testing uses scripts and tools for testing. Manual testing is suitable for exploratory, usability, and ad-hoc testing, while automated testing is efficient for regression testing, load testing, and repetitive test cases.

Question 3: How does performance testing differ from functional testing, and what objectives does it aim to achieve?
Answer: Performance testing evaluates the software's responsiveness, stability, and scalability under different loads and conditions, while functional testing ensures that the software's features and functions work as expected. The

objectives of performance testing include assessing system performance, identifying bottlenecks, and optimizing software for better user experiences.

Question 4: What is the significance of security testing in software development, and how does it help in achieving software testing objectives?
Answer: Security testing assesses the software for vulnerabilities and potential threats to data and privacy. It is crucial because it helps ensure that the software is resistant to attacks, protecting sensitive information and maintaining the integrity of the application.

Question 5: Can you provide an example of a situation where applying a specific type of software testing was essential in identifying a critical issue and ensuring software reliability?
Answer: In a financial software application, applying penetration testing (a type of security testing) identified a critical vulnerability that could have exposed sensitive customer data to external threats. Addressing this issue in a timely manner prevented a potential security breach, protecting the organization and its customers.

10.3 Seven Principles of software testing

Question 1: What are the Seven Principles of software testing, and why are they fundamental to the testing process?
Answer: The Seven Principles of software testing are: testing shows the presence of defects, exhaustive testing is impossible, early testing, defect clustering, the pesticide paradox, testing is context-dependent, and absence-of-errors fallacy. These principles are fundamental as they guide testers in making informed decisions, setting realistic expectations, and optimizing testing efforts.

Question 2: How does the principle of "exhaustive testing is impossible" impact the testing process, and what strategies are employed to address it?
Answer: This principle recognizes that testing all possible scenarios is impractical. Testers address it by using risk-based testing, prioritizing test cases based on potential impact, and focusing on critical areas of the software where defects are more likely to occur.

Question 3: What is the significance of the "early testing" principle, and how does it contribute to the overall software quality?
Answer: Early testing emphasizes starting the testing process as soon as possible in the software development lifecycle. It's significant because it allows defects to be identified and addressed at an early stage when they are less expensive and time-consuming to fix, leading to higher software quality.

Question 4: Can you explain the "defect clustering" principle and provide an example of how it has been observed in software testing?
Answer: Defect clustering suggests that a small number of modules or functions typically contain the majority of defects. For example, in a large software application, it's common to find that a specific component or module consistently exhibits more defects than others, emphasizing the need for more rigorous testing in that area.

Question 5: How does the "testing is context-dependent" principle influence the testing approach, and why is it important to consider the context of each project?
Answer: This principle recognizes that the testing process should be adapted to the specific context of each project, including its goals, requirements, and constraints. It's important because testing strategies may vary based on the project's unique characteristics, such as its industry, technology, and objectives, ensuring the most effective and relevant testing methods are applied.

10.4 Testing Guidelines

Question 1: What are Testing Guidelines, and why are they important in the software testing process?
Answer: Testing Guidelines are a set of rules and best practices that provide direction for effective testing. They are important because they help ensure consistency in the testing process, improve test coverage, and increase the likelihood of detecting defects.

Question 2: Can you explain the significance of clear and detailed test documentation as part of testing guidelines?
Answer: Clear and detailed test documentation, as recommended by testing guidelines, ensures that test cases, test data, and expected results are well-documented. This is crucial for test repeatability, understanding test scope, and making it easier for different team members to execute and maintain tests.

Question 3: How do testing guidelines address the need for a structured and organized approach to test planning and execution?
Answer: Testing guidelines emphasize structured test planning, test case design, and test execution to ensure that testing activities are systematic and organized. A structured approach helps in managing testing tasks, tracking progress, and effectively communicating test results.

Question 4: What role does collaboration and communication play in adhering to testing guidelines, and how does it impact the testing process?
Answer: Collaboration and communication are essential aspects of testing guidelines, promoting teamwork and information sharing among testing teams, development teams, and stakeholders. Effective collaboration ensures that all parties are aligned on testing objectives, priorities, and results, leading to improved testing outcomes.

Question 5: Can you provide an example of how adherence to testing guidelines led to a more successful testing phase in a software project?
Answer: In a software project, following testing guidelines resulted in improved test planning and communication. By involving all stakeholders in the testing process, clarifying roles and responsibilities, and documenting test procedures meticulously, the project team was able to execute tests more efficiently, detect defects early, and significantly reduce post-release issues, ultimately leading to a more successful software deployment.

10.5 White Box and Black Box Testing

Question 1: What is White Box Testing and Black Box Testing, and how do they differ in terms of their approaches and objectives?
Answer: White Box Testing focuses on the internal structure and logic of the software, testing code paths and system behavior. Black Box Testing, on the other hand, tests the software's functionality without considering its internal workings. White Box Testing aims to identify defects and vulnerabilities in the code, while Black Box Testing aims to ensure the software meets its specified requirements.

Question 2: How do White Box and Black Box Testing contribute to a comprehensive testing strategy, and when is each type typically applied in the software development lifecycle?
Answer: White Box Testing is essential for early detection of code-level issues and vulnerabilities. It is often applied during unit testing and code review phases. Black Box Testing complements this by validating the software from an end-user perspective, typically performed during system and acceptance testing.

Question 3: What types of defects or issues are more likely to be identified through White Box Testing, and what are some typical test techniques used in this approach?
Answer: White Box Testing is effective at identifying code-level issues like logic errors, incorrect conditional statements, and security vulnerabilities. Techniques include code reviews, path testing, and statement coverage testing.

Question 4: Can you explain the concept of equivalence partitioning and boundary value analysis in the context of Black Box Testing, and why are these techniques valuable?
Answer: Equivalence partitioning and boundary value analysis are techniques used in Black Box Testing to define test cases based on input partitions and boundary conditions. They help ensure test cases are representative of typical user scenarios and critical edge cases, increasing the likelihood of identifying defects and issues.

Question 5: How does the choice between White Box and Black Box Testing depend on project requirements, goals, and constraints, and can both approaches be used in the same testing effort?
Answer: The choice between White Box and Black Box Testing depends on project objectives, constraints, and the nature of the application. In many cases, both approaches are used in the same testing effort to provide a well-rounded

assessment of the software. White Box Testing helps identify internal code issues, while Black Box Testing ensures the software meets its functional and usability requirements.

10.6 Levels of Testing

10.6.1 Unit Testing

Question 1: What is the main purpose of Unit Testing, and why is it considered an integral part of the development process?
Answer 1: The main purpose of Unit Testing is to verify that individual units or components of the software work as intended. It's essential in identifying and fixing code-level issues early in the development cycle, ensuring each unit functions correctly.

Question 2: How do you approach Unit Testing for complex functions or methods, and what are some best practices for designing effective unit test cases?
Answer 2: For complex functions, I break them down into smaller, testable units. Best practices include testing a range of inputs, handling edge cases, and using testing frameworks and assertions to validate results.

Question 3: Can you explain the concept of Test-Driven Development (TDD) and its relationship with Unit Testing?
Answer 3: Test-Driven Development (TDD) involves writing tests before code implementation. Unit Testing plays a significant role in TDD as it guides the development process, ensuring that code meets specific test cases.

Question 4: What tools and frameworks do you commonly use for Unit Testing, and how do they aid in automating the testing process?
Answer 4: I often use testing frameworks like JUnit for Java or NUnit for .NET. These frameworks provide a structured environment for creating and executing unit tests, automating test execution and reporting.

Question 5: Can you explain the difference between mocking and stubbing in Unit Testing, and when would you use each technique?
Answer 5: Mocking involves creating objects that simulate dependencies, while stubbing replaces real methods with controlled behavior. I use mocking when I want to verify interactions, and stubbing when I need specific return values from dependencies in isolation.

10.6.2 System Testing

Question 1: What is the primary objective of System Testing, and how does it differ from Unit Testing?
Answer 1: The primary objective of System Testing is to ensure that the entire software system works as a cohesive whole. Unlike Unit Testing, which focuses on individual components, System Testing evaluates the system's functionality and interactions.

Question 2: How do you design test cases for System Testing, and what factors influence the selection of test scenarios and data?
Answer 2: Test cases for System Testing are based on system requirements and user scenarios. I consider factors like user inputs, system configurations, and critical use cases to ensure comprehensive coverage.

Question 3: What types of testing techniques are commonly used in System Testing, and how do they help uncover issues in the integrated system?
Answer 3: Techniques like functional testing, performance testing, and security testing are commonly used in System Testing. Functional testing ensures requirements are met, performance testing assesses system speed and scalability, and security testing identifies vulnerabilities.

Question 4: Can you explain the significance of end-to-end testing in System Testing, and how does it ensure that the entire system functions as expected?

Answer 4: End-to-end testing evaluates the entire workflow of a system, from user input to final output. It helps identify issues that may arise due to interactions between different components, ensuring the entire system functions cohesively.

Question 5: What is the role of regression testing in System Testing, and how do you manage and prioritize regression test suites effectively?
Answer 5: Regression testing in System Testing ensures that new features or changes do not introduce new defects or affect existing functionality. I manage regression test suites by prioritizing critical test cases, automating where possible, and running tests incrementally to save time.

10.6.3 Integration Testing

Question 1: What is the primary focus of Integration Testing, and how does it differ from System Testing?
Answer 1: Integration Testing focuses on evaluating the interactions between different modules or components of the software. It differs from System Testing, which examines the entire system's functionality and behavior.

Question 2: How do you identify and resolve issues discovered during Integration Testing, and what strategies do you use to isolate integration-related defects?
Answer 2: Issues identified in Integration Testing are often due to component interactions. I use techniques like top-down, bottom-up, or incremental integration testing to isolate defects and then debug and fix them at the integration points.

Question 3: Can you explain the concept of stubs and drivers in Integration Testing, and how do they facilitate testing in a component-based system?
Answer 3: Stubs simulate lower-level components, while drivers simulate higher-level components. They allow testing of components that are yet to be integrated, ensuring that each component can be tested independently.

Question 4: How does integration testing help in validating data flow and error handling between software modules, and what are the typical challenges you may encounter during this process?
Answer 4: Integration Testing validates data flow and error handling across module boundaries, ensuring smooth communication. Challenges can include missing interface specifications, communication issues, and identifying the source of defects in complex integrations.

Question 5: In what scenarios would you choose a top-down integration testing approach, and when would a bottom-up approach be more suitable?
Answer 5: I choose a top-down approach when critical higher-level modules are ready for testing. A bottom-up approach is suitable when lower-level modules are stable, allowing early integration testing and defect identification. The choice depends on project priorities and component readiness.

10.6.4 Acceptance Testing

Question 1: What is Acceptance Testing, and why is it a crucial phase in the software development process?
Answer 1: Acceptance Testing is the final phase of testing where end-users or stakeholders verify that the software aligns with business needs and objectives. It's crucial to ensure that the software is ready for production use and meets the requirements set by the client or business.

Question 2: What are the key differences between User Acceptance Testing (UAT) and System Acceptance Testing (SAT), and when are they typically performed?
Answer 2: User Acceptance Testing (UAT) involves end-users testing the software, while System Acceptance Testing (SAT) is performed by a specialized testing team. UAT is typically conducted in the later stages of the software development cycle, while SAT is done earlier.

Question 3: How do you design effective test cases for Acceptance Testing, and what criteria are essential to meet for the software to pass acceptance tests?

Answer 3: Effective test cases for Acceptance Testing are designed based on business requirements and user scenarios. Criteria for passing acceptance tests include meeting user expectations, functionality, and performance, and ensuring compliance with business goals.

Question 4: Can you explain the role of Alpha and Beta Testing in the context of Acceptance Testing, and how they involve end-users?
Answer 4: Alpha Testing involves internal users and is performed within the organization. Beta Testing involves external users who test the software in a real-world environment. Both Alpha and Beta Testing are forms of Acceptance Testing where end-users provide valuable feedback.

Question 5: How does Acceptance Testing contribute to the overall software quality and user satisfaction, and can you share an example where it led to a successful software deployment?
Answer 5: Acceptance Testing ensures that the software aligns with user needs and business objectives. When done effectively, it enhances user satisfaction, reduces post-release issues, and leads to a successful software deployment. For example, in an e-commerce project, thorough UAT ensured that the checkout process met user expectations, resulting in higher sales and customer satisfaction.

10.6.5 Alpha Testing

Question 1: What is Alpha Testing, and how does it differ from other testing phases?
Answer 1: Alpha Testing is an early phase of testing where internal users evaluate the software's functionality and usability. It differs from other phases by involving a select group of users within the organization who have access to the software's early versions.

Question 2: How can you select the right participants for Alpha Testing, and what are the benefits of this approach in identifying issues and improvements?
Answer 2: Participants for Alpha Testing should represent the target user group and have a diverse range of skills. The benefits of Alpha Testing include identifying defects and usability issues early, improving the software, and ensuring it aligns with user expectations.

Question 3: Can you describe the typical Alpha Testing process, from planning and execution to feedback incorporation and retesting?
Answer 3: Alpha Testing starts with planning, participant selection, and test case design. Testing is carried out, and feedback is collected. Incorporating feedback and retesting are essential to refine the software based on the results of Alpha Testing.

Question 4: What are the key challenges in Alpha Testing, and how can they be addressed to ensure its success?
Answer 4: Challenges in Alpha Testing include the limited number of participants and the potential for biased feedback. These challenges can be addressed by diversifying the participant group, setting clear expectations, and using objective criteria to evaluate the software.

Question 5: Can you provide an example of a situation where Alpha Testing led to the identification and resolution of significant issues, improving the software's quality and user experience?
Answer 5: In a software project, Alpha Testing revealed a critical issue in the user registration process, preventing users from completing the registration form. By addressing this issue early in the development cycle, the software was enhanced, and the user experience significantly improved, resulting in a successful product launch.

10.6.6 Beta Testing

Question 1: What is Beta Testing, and how does it involve external users in the software evaluation process?
Answer 1: Beta Testing is the phase where a select group of external users are invited to test the software in their real-world environments. It allows developers to gather feedback from diverse user perspectives.

Question 2: How can you recruit and select appropriate participants for Beta Testing, and what criteria should they meet? Answer 2: Participants for Beta Testing should represent the target audience, have varying levels of expertise, and use the software in different scenarios. Selection criteria include demographics, skills, and the ability to provide constructive feedback.

Question 3: Can you explain the benefits of conducting Beta Testing, and how does it contribute to software quality and user satisfaction?
Answer 3: Beta Testing helps identify real-world issues, usability problems, and edge cases that internal testing may miss. It leads to improved software quality, increased user satisfaction, and greater confidence in the product.

Question 4: What is the role of Beta Testers in reporting defects and providing feedback, and how should their feedback be incorporated into the software development process?
Answer 4: Beta Testers play a crucial role in reporting defects and providing feedback. Their feedback should be carefully analyzed, prioritized, and incorporated into the software development process to enhance the product based on user needs.

Question 5: Can you share an example of a successful Beta Testing phase that resulted in valuable user feedback and ultimately led to a more refined and user-friendly software product?
Answer 5: In a mobile app project, Beta Testers provided feedback on a user interface issue related to button placement. The development team made the necessary adjustments based on this feedback, resulting in an improved interface and a highly rated app upon its official release.

10.6.7 Regression Testing

Question 1: What is Regression Testing, and why is it essential in the software development lifecycle?
Answer 1: Regression Testing is the process of retesting a software application to ensure that recent code changes have not introduced new defects or negatively impacted existing functionality. It is essential to maintain software quality and stability.

Question 2: How can you create an effective set of regression test cases, and what considerations should be taken into account when selecting test cases for regression testing?
Answer 2: Effective regression test cases should cover critical functionality and areas most likely to be affected by code changes. Considerations include prioritizing high-impact test cases, selecting test cases that represent typical user scenarios, and ensuring comprehensive test coverage.

Question 3: Can you explain the difference between complete and partial regression testing, and when would you choose one over the other?
Answer 3: Complete regression testing involves executing all existing test cases, while partial regression testing selects a subset of test cases based on changes. Complete regression testing is suitable when there are doubts about the impact of changes, while partial regression testing is chosen to save time and resources when changes are minor.

Question 4: What are the challenges associated with maintaining an effective regression test suite, and how can you address them to ensure efficiency and coverage?
Answer 4: Challenges include the growth of the test suite and test maintenance costs. These can be addressed by regularly reviewing and updating test cases, automating repetitive tests, and leveraging test management tools to track changes and coverage.

Question 5: Can you provide an example where thorough regression testing prevented a post-release defect, ultimately leading to a more reliable and stable software product?
Answer 5: In a web application project, a code change inadvertently affected the payment processing functionality. Thorough regression testing identified the issue, allowing it to be fixed before the software was released, preventing potential financial losses and maintaining the software's reliability.

10.7 Debugging

Question 1: What is debugging, and why is it a critical process in software development?
Answer 1: Debugging is the process of identifying and fixing defects, errors, or unexpected behavior in software code. It is critical because it ensures that the software functions correctly, leading to a high-quality product.

Question 2: Can you explain the difference between debugging tools and techniques, and how do they assist in the debugging process?
Answer 2: Debugging tools are software applications that help identify and track issues, while debugging techniques are methodologies for finding and fixing defects. Tools like debuggers, profilers, and IDEs support various techniques such as breakpoint analysis, code inspection, and trace analysis.

Question 3: What are the common challenges in debugging, and how can software developers effectively overcome them?
Answer 3: Common challenges in debugging include pinpointing the root cause of defects and managing the debugging process efficiently. Developers can overcome these challenges by using systematic debugging approaches, documenting issues, and collaborating with team members for problem-solving.

Question 4: How does the process of remote debugging work, and what are the benefits of this approach in a distributed software development environment?
Answer 4: Remote debugging allows developers to debug software running on a remote server or device from their local development environment. It is beneficial in distributed environments as it reduces the need for physical access to remote systems, making debugging more efficient and collaborative.

Question 5: Can you provide an example of a challenging debugging situation you've encountered and how you successfully resolved it?
Answer 5: In a web application project, I faced a complex issue where user data was not being saved correctly in the database. After extensive debugging, I discovered that a data transformation function had a subtle bug. By carefully examining the code and its execution flow, I was able to identify and fix the issue, resulting in accurate data storage and a successful resolution of the problem.

Online Resources

Chapter 10 YouTube Playlist Link:
Link: https://www.youtube.com/playlist?list=PLzlh_31VWEFoFGTiNRypX3swnvzQCEqdY
QR Code:

Online Exam Paper Link:
Link: https://forms.gle/f9znsd1x5XeNXVwZ7
QR Code:

MCQ Video Playlist Link:
Link: https://youtu.be/uqPIKKWlbyY
QR Code:

True/False Video Playlist Link:
Link: https://youtu.be/poENiWKUnlM
QR Code:

Online MCQ Exam Paper Link:
Link: https://forms.office.com/r/xdB2BLDuMS
QR Code:

Online True/False Exam Paper Link:
Link: https://forms.office.com/r/epLmQ1vLHi
QR Code:

Chapter 11: Software Verification and Validation

11.1 Introduction

Question 1: What is the difference between Software Verification and Software Validation, and why are they both essential in the software development process?
Answer 1: Software Verification ensures that the software is developed correctly according to the specified requirements, while Software Validation confirms that it meets the user's actual needs. Both processes are essential for delivering a high-quality software product that aligns with requirements and user expectations.

Question 2: Can you explain the key activities involved in Software Verification and Validation, and how do they contribute to software quality?
Answer 2: Software Verification activities include code reviews, inspections, and unit testing, aiming to identify defects early in the development process. Software Validation involves system testing, user acceptance testing, and usability testing to confirm that the software satisfies user needs and performs as expected, contributing to overall software quality.

Question 3: What role does Testing play in Software Verification and Validation, and how can different testing types be applied to these processes?
Answer 3: Testing is a crucial component of both Verification and Validation. Unit testing and Integration testing are commonly used in Verification, while System testing and Acceptance testing are integral to Validation. Each testing type ensures that different aspects of the software are checked for correctness and user satisfaction.

Question 4: How can you ensure that Software Verification and Validation activities are thorough and systematic, and what are some best practices to follow?
Answer 4: To ensure thorough Verification and Validation, it's essential to follow established test plans, create comprehensive test cases, and involve different team members in the process. Best practices include continuous review of requirements, maintaining clear documentation, and using test automation where applicable.

Question 5: Can you share an example from your experience where effective Software Verification and Validation processes led to the successful delivery of a high-quality software product?
Answer 5: In a healthcare software project, rigorous Verification and Validation processes were applied to ensure compliance with medical regulations. This resulted in the early detection of critical defects and the confirmation that the software met stringent user requirements. The project was successfully delivered, providing a reliable and compliant software solution for healthcare providers.

11.2 Role of Verification and Verification in SDLC

Question 1: What is the primary role of Verification in the SDLC, and how does it contribute to the development process?
Answer 1: The primary role of Verification in the SDLC is to ensure that the software is built correctly according to the specified requirements. It involves activities such as code reviews, inspections, and unit testing to identify and rectify defects early in the development process, promoting code quality and reliability.

Question 2: What is the primary role of Validation in the SDLC, and how does it contribute to the overall success of the software project?
Answer 2: The primary role of Validation in the SDLC is to confirm that the software meets the user's actual needs and performs as expected in its intended environment. It involves activities like system testing, user acceptance testing, and usability testing to ensure that the software satisfies user requirements and delivers a high-quality user experience, contributing to the project's success.

Question 3: How do Verification and Validation activities work in tandem throughout the SDLC, and how does this collaborative approach enhance software quality?

Answer 3: Verification activities (e.g., unit testing, code reviews) ensure that the software is built correctly, while Validation activities (e.g., user acceptance testing) confirm that it meets user needs. By working together, Verification identifies defects early, which are then validated for their impact on user requirements, ultimately enhancing software quality and alignment with both technical and user perspectives.

Question 4: What challenges can arise when implementing Verification and Validation in the SDLC, and how can they be effectively addressed?
Answer 4: Challenges may include resource constraints, communication gaps, and the complexity of testing. These challenges can be addressed by allocating adequate resources, fostering collaboration among team members, using well-defined test plans, and embracing test automation to streamline the process.

Question 5: Can you provide an example from your experience where the effective implementation of Verification and Validation played a significant role in the successful delivery of a software project?
Answer 5: In a financial software project, rigorous Verification activities ensured that the core financial calculations were accurate. Validation activities, including user acceptance testing by financial experts, confirmed that the software met their specific financial reporting requirements. This comprehensive approach led to a successful project outcome, with a high-quality financial software solution that met user needs and regulatory standards.

11.3 Difference between Verification Validation

Question 1: What is the fundamental difference between Verification and Validation in the software development process?
Answer 1: The fundamental difference is that Verification focuses on ensuring that the software is developed correctly, according to the specified requirements, while Validation focuses on confirming that the software meets the user's actual needs and performs as expected.

Question 2: Can you provide examples that illustrate the distinction between Verification and Validation activities in software development?
Answer 2: Certainly. A code review, which is a Verification activity, checks the code against coding standards and requirements to catch syntax errors. In contrast, User Acceptance Testing (UAT), which is a Validation activity, evaluates the software from the user's perspective to ensure it aligns with their expectations.

Question 3: How do Verification and Validation activities complement each other in the software development life cycle?
Answer 3: Verification activities (e.g., code inspections, unit testing) ensure that the software is built correctly, while Validation activities (e.g., system testing, user acceptance testing) confirm that it satisfies user requirements. Together, they provide a comprehensive approach to deliver a high-quality software product.

Question 4: In the event of a discrepancy between the specified requirements and the user's expectations, how would you address it in the Verification and Validation process?
Answer 4: In such a scenario, Verification identifies the deviation from the specified requirements, and Validation confirms that it aligns with the user's expectations. The development team would then need to reconcile the discrepancies by adjusting the software to meet both the specified requirements and user needs.

Question 5: Why is it important to maintain a clear distinction between Verification and Validation activities in software development, and how does this contribute to successful project outcomes?
Answer 5: Maintaining a clear distinction is vital because it ensures that both technical and user-centric aspects of the software are thoroughly evaluated. This distinction helps in identifying defects early, aligning the software with requirements, and delivering a product that meets user expectations, ultimately leading to successful project outcomes.

11.4 Software Maintenance

Question 1: What is Software Maintenance, and why is it a crucial phase in the software development life cycle?
Answer 1: Software Maintenance refers to the process of modifying and enhancing existing software to meet evolving needs, fix defects, and ensure its continued functionality. It is crucial to extend the software's lifespan, improve its performance, and adapt it to changing user requirements.

Question 2: Can you explain the various types of Software Maintenance, such as Corrective, Adaptive, Perfective, and Preventive, and provide examples of each?
Answer 2: Corrective Maintenance addresses defects and bugs, ensuring the software functions as intended. Adaptive Maintenance involves modifying the software to accommodate changes in the environment. Perfective Maintenance aims to improve software performance and usability. Preventive Maintenance proactively reduces the risk of future issues through updates and enhancements.

Question 3: What are the key challenges associated with Software Maintenance, and how can organizations effectively manage and mitigate these challenges?
Answer 3: Challenges include managing a growing codebase, understanding legacy systems, and maintaining documentation. Effective management involves using version control systems, establishing clear coding standards, and investing in knowledge transfer to ensure a smooth transition when maintaining legacy software.

Question 4: How does Software Maintenance contribute to the overall success and longevity of a software product, and can you provide an example where effective maintenance led to significant improvements?
Answer 4: Software Maintenance extends the product's lifespan, adapts it to changing needs, and prevents issues from impacting users. An example would be a mobile app receiving regular updates to add new features, improve performance, and fix bugs, resulting in increased user satisfaction and a longer software lifespan.

Question 5: In your experience, how do you prioritize and plan for Software Maintenance tasks, especially when dealing with competing demands and limited resources?
Answer 5: Prioritization involves assessing the impact of maintenance tasks on the software's performance and user experience. Tasks that address critical defects or security vulnerabilities are prioritized first. Effective planning includes creating a maintenance schedule, allocating resources, and defining clear objectives for each maintenance phase.

11.4.1 Types of Maintenance (Corrective, Adaptive, Perfective)

Question 1 (Corrective Maintenance): Can you explain what Corrective Maintenance is and provide an example of a situation where it's required in software maintenance?
Answer 1: Corrective Maintenance involves fixing defects and errors in software. An example would be patching a critical security vulnerability in a web application to prevent unauthorized access or data breaches.

Question 2 (Adaptive Maintenance): What is Adaptive Maintenance, and when is it typically needed in the software maintenance cycle?
Answer 2: Adaptive Maintenance involves modifying software to adapt to changes in its environment. It's needed when, for instance, an e-commerce website must be updated to comply with new regulations or integrate with a new payment gateway.

Question 3 (Perfective Maintenance): How does Perfective Maintenance contribute to the overall improvement of software, and can you provide an example where it led to significant enhancements?
Answer 3: Perfective Maintenance focuses on enhancing software performance and usability. An example would be optimizing the code of a video editing software to reduce rendering times, leading to a more efficient user experience.

Question 4 (Combining Maintenance Types): Can you describe a scenario where a software maintenance project required a combination of Corrective, Adaptive, and Perfective maintenance activities?
Answer 4: Certainly. In a mobile app project, Corrective Maintenance fixed crash issues (bugs), Adaptive Maintenance adapted the app to new OS updates, and Perfective Maintenance improved the user interface for better user experience—all in a single project.

Question 5 (Prioritizing Maintenance Types): How do you prioritize between Corrective, Adaptive, and Perfective maintenance when resources are limited, and there are competing demands?
Answer 5: Prioritization depends on factors like the impact on users, compliance requirements, and business objectives. Corrective maintenance addressing critical defects and security issues typically takes precedence, followed by Adaptive and Perfective maintenance based on the project's specific needs.

11.4.2 Characteristics of Quality Software

Question 1: What are the key characteristics of quality software, and why are they important for both developers and end-users?
Answer 1: Quality software is characterized by reliability, performance, usability, security, and maintainability. These characteristics are essential for developers to create robust software and for end-users to have a positive and productive experience.

Question 2: How does reliability play a crucial role in defining the quality of software, and can you share an example where reliability was a critical factor in software development?
Answer 2: Reliability ensures that software consistently performs as expected. For instance, in a financial application, reliability is paramount to prevent financial losses due to software failures, making it a critical factor in development.

Question 3: What is the significance of usability in quality software, and how can user-friendly design impact the overall success of a software product?
Answer 3: Usability is vital for user satisfaction and productivity. A well-designed, user-friendly interface can lead to higher adoption rates and user retention, making it a key driver of a software product's success.

Question 4: How does security contribute to the quality of software, and can you provide an example where a security breach highlighted the importance of software security?
Answer 4: Security is crucial to protect user data and prevent vulnerabilities. An example would be a data breach in a healthcare software system, emphasizing the importance of robust security measures to safeguard sensitive patient information.

Question 5: Why is maintainability a key characteristic of quality software, and how does it affect the long-term success and cost-effectiveness of software projects?
Answer 5: Maintainability ensures that software can be easily updated and adapted. It reduces long-term costs and effort in software maintenance and enhancements. For example, in a content management system, maintainability allows for effortless content updates and system expansions, ensuring cost-effectiveness.

11.4.3 Techniques for Software Maintenance

1. Question: What are the key challenges associated with software maintenance, and how do you address them?
Answer: Software maintenance can be challenging due to evolving requirements, bug fixes, and changing technology. To address these challenges, we use techniques like impact analysis to assess changes, version control systems to track modifications, and regression testing to ensure new updates don't introduce defects.

2. Question: Can you explain the concept of "refactoring" in software maintenance, and how does it contribute to improving software quality?
Answer: Refactoring involves restructuring code to enhance its readability and maintainability without changing its external behavior. It's a proactive technique that helps prevent software decay, making the codebase more manageable and efficient, ultimately improving software quality.

3. Question: What role does documentation play in software maintenance, and how can it aid the process?
Answer: Documentation is crucial in understanding the software's architecture, functions, and dependencies. It aids in diagnosing issues, making enhancements, and ensuring knowledge transfer. Effective documentation practices include code comments, inline explanations, and maintaining updated user manuals.

4. Question: What is regression testing, and how does it ensure that software maintenance changes don't introduce new defects?
Answer: Regression testing is a technique that involves retesting the software to ensure that new changes or modifications do not adversely impact existing functionality. It uses automated test cases to verify that the software still behaves as expected, helping detect and prevent regression defects.

5. Question: How do you prioritize software maintenance tasks when faced with limited resources and tight schedules?
Answer: Prioritization in software maintenance involves assessing the impact of changes or defects on the software's functionality and criticality. We use techniques such as the MoSCoW method (Must, Should, Could, and Won't) to prioritize tasks based on their importance, ensuring that critical issues are addressed first within resource constraints.

Online Resources

Chapter 11 YouTube Playlist Link:
Link: https://www.youtube.com/playlist?list=PLzlh_31VWEFp-MPUQG8kjY2CcpclIMc7q
QR Code:

Online Exam Paper Link:
Link: https://forms.gle/vrRKkZWm7P29si9p8
QR Code:

MCQ Video Playlist Link:
Link: https://youtu.be/TM120fmU0LE
QR Code:

True/False Video Playlist Link:
Link: https://youtu.be/T7rO5Si8cvQ
QR Code:

Online MCQ Exam Paper Link:
Link: https://forms.office.com/r/APAphk0jtT
QR Code:

Online True/False Exam Paper Link:
Link: https://forms.office.com/r/7G2kmZv7YJ
QR Code:

Chapter 12: Unified Modeling Language (UML)

12.1 Introduction to UML

Question 1: What is UML, and why is it essential in software engineering?
Answer 1: UML, or Unified Modeling Language, is a standardized language for visualizing, designing, and documenting software systems. It is essential in software engineering because it provides a common visual framework that aids in communication, design, and documentation, promoting effective collaboration among stakeholders.

Question 2: How does UML benefit software development projects?
Answer 2: UML benefits software development by offering a consistent and visual way to represent system structure and behavior. It helps in clarifying requirements, designing system architectures, and documenting complex software, making it easier for teams to understand and work on projects.

Question 3: Can you explain the primary goals of UML in software engineering?
Answer 3: The primary goals of UML are to facilitate effective communication among project stakeholders, enhance software design and development, and provide a standardized means for documenting software systems. It promotes clear and concise modeling of complex systems.

Question 4: In what scenarios is UML particularly useful, and how does it support better project management?
Answer 4: UML is particularly useful in complex software projects, especially those involving multiple team members and stakeholders. It supports project management by providing a shared understanding of the system's structure and behavior, enabling better planning, decision-making, and risk management.

Question 5: How does UML help bridge the communication gap between technical and non-technical stakeholders in a software project?
Answer 5: UML uses visual notations and diagrams that are easily understood by both technical and non-technical stakeholders. It provides a common language for discussing software requirements, design, and functionality, ensuring that all parties can effectively contribute to the project's success.

12.2 Basic Structures and Modeling Classes

Question 1: What is the primary purpose of UML class diagrams, and how do they contribute to software modeling?
Answer 1: UML class diagrams serve to visualize and document the static structure of a software system. They help in modeling the system's components, their attributes, and their relationships, providing a blueprint for system design and development.

Question 2: Can you explain the key components of a UML class diagram and their roles in representing a software system?
Answer 2: A UML class diagram includes classes, attributes, operations, and relationships. Classes represent the system's entities, attributes define their properties, operations describe their behavior, and relationships illustrate how classes interact and collaborate within the system.

Question 3: How does UML differentiate between classes and objects, and why is this distinction important?
Answer 3: In UML, classes are templates that define the structure and behavior shared by multiple objects. Objects, on the other hand, are instances of classes with specific data and state. This distinction is vital as it allows for the modeling of reusable design patterns and relationships.

Question 4: What is the significance of associations and their role in UML class diagrams?
Answer 4: Associations in UML class diagrams represent relationships between classes. They are essential for modeling how classes collaborate and interact within a software system. Associations provide a way to depict connections, dependencies, and collaborations among different classes.

Question 5: How can UML class diagrams aid in software design and development, and in what ways do they improve team collaboration?
Answer 5: UML class diagrams support software design and development by providing a visual representation of the system's structure, enabling developers to better plan and implement the software. They enhance team collaboration by offering a common language and visual framework that fosters clear communication among team members and stakeholders.

12.3 Common Modeling Techniques

Question 1: What is the purpose of UML use case diagrams, and how do they aid in defining software requirements?
Answer 1: UML use case diagrams help in defining the functional requirements of a software system by visualizing how external actors interact with the system and the specific functionalities the system must provide to meet user needs.

Question 2: What are activity diagrams in UML, and in what scenarios are they most beneficial for modeling system behavior?
Answer 2: Activity diagrams in UML are used to model the workflow and processes within a system. They are particularly beneficial for visualizing complex business processes, demonstrating how different activities are performed, and illustrating the flow of control within the system.

Question 3: How do sequence diagrams in UML differ from collaboration diagrams, and when would you choose one over the other?
Answer 3: Sequence diagrams focus on depicting the interactions between objects or components in specific scenarios or during particular operations, making them ideal for understanding the dynamic behavior of a system. Collaboration diagrams, on the other hand, provide an overview of the structural organization of objects and how they collaborate. The choice depends on whether you need to emphasize behavior or structure.

Question 4: What is the primary goal of modeling relationships between classes in UML, and how can it enhance software design?
Answer 4: Modeling relationships between classes in UML is crucial for representing how classes interact and collaborate within a software system. It enhances software design by ensuring that the system's structure and behavior are accurately depicted, enabling better decision-making and design planning.

Question 5: How do UML modeling techniques, such as use case diagrams and activity diagrams, contribute to effective communication between project stakeholders?
Answer 5: UML modeling techniques provide visual representations that are easily understood by both technical and non-technical stakeholders. They foster effective communication by offering a common language for discussing system requirements, behavior, and functionality, ensuring that all project stakeholders can participate in discussions and decision-making.

12.4 Relationships and Mechanisms

Question 1: Can you explain what associations are in UML, and how they are used to depict relationships between classes?
Answer 1: In UML, associations represent relationships between classes. They show how classes are connected and interact within a system. Associations are essential for modeling collaboration, dependencies, and communication between classes.

Question 2: What is the difference between aggregation and composition in UML, and when should you use each of these relationship types?
Answer 2: Aggregation and composition are two types of associations. Aggregation represents a "whole-part" relationship, where the "part" class can exist independently of the "whole." Composition, on the other hand, signifies a stronger relationship, where the "part" class cannot exist without the "whole." The choice depends on the strength and permanence of the relationship.

Question 3: How does generalization and inheritance work in UML, and what is their significance in modeling class hierarchies?
Answer 3: Generalization and inheritance are mechanisms in UML that establish an "is-a" relationship between classes. Generalization allows you to create a more general superclass from specific subclasses, inheriting attributes and behaviors. They are significant for building class hierarchies, ensuring that subclasses inherit common properties and behaviors from their superclass.

Question 4: When designing UML class diagrams, why is it crucial to accurately represent relationships and mechanisms between classes?
Answer 4: Accurate representation of relationships and mechanisms in UML class diagrams is essential for a clear and comprehensive understanding of how classes collaborate and interact within a software system. It supports effective communication, design, and documentation, which are critical for successful software development.

Question 5: Can you provide an example of a real-world scenario where UML associations, aggregations, or compositions played a crucial role in modeling relationships between classes?
Answer 5: Consider an e-commerce system where the "Order" class aggregates "OrderItem" classes to represent items within an order. This aggregation signifies that an order consists of items, but the items can exist independently. It's a real-world example of using UML relationships to model a "whole-part" relationship in software.

12.5 Class Diagrams

Question 1: What is the primary purpose of UML class diagrams, and how do they benefit software design and development?
Answer 1: UML class diagrams are primarily used to depict the static structure of a software system. They benefit software design and development by providing a visual representation of the system's architecture, including classes, attributes, operations, and their relationships. This helps in better planning and implementation of software projects.

Question 2: How do you represent attributes and operations in a UML class diagram, and what is their significance in modeling classes?
Answer 2: Attributes are represented as properties within classes, while operations are depicted with method signatures. Attributes define the properties of a class, and operations describe its behavior. They play a critical role in modeling the characteristics and functionality of classes within the system.

Question 3: What types of relationships can exist between classes in UML class diagrams, and how do they impact the system's design?
Answer 3: Classes in UML class diagrams can have various relationships, including associations, aggregations, compositions, and generalization. These relationships define how classes interact, collaborate, and inherit properties. They impact the design by providing insights into the structure and behavior of the software system.

Question 4: Can you provide an example of a real-world scenario where UML class diagrams have been used to model software systems effectively?
Answer 4: In an online banking application, UML class diagrams can represent classes like "Account," "Transaction," and "Customer." They show how accounts are associated with transactions, customers own accounts, and transactions affect account balances, providing a clear view of the software's structural and functional aspects.

Question 5: How does UML class diagram modeling contribute to improved communication and collaboration among software development teams and stakeholders?
Answer 5: UML class diagrams provide a visual and standardized way to represent a system's structure. They enhance communication by offering a common language that technical and non-technical stakeholders can understand. This clarity fosters effective collaboration, ensuring that everyone has a shared vision of the software system.

12.6 Advanced Structured Modeling

Question 1: What is the role of behavioral modeling in UML, and how does it enhance our understanding of a software system?

Answer 1: Behavioral modeling in UML focuses on representing the dynamic aspects of a system, such as how objects or components interact over time. It enhances our understanding by illustrating the system's behavior during different scenarios, providing insights into its functioning.

Question 2: Can you explain the significance of state diagrams in UML, and provide an example of when they are valuable in software modeling?
Answer 2: State diagrams are used to depict the behavior of an object or system in response to various stimuli and conditions. They are valuable in modeling systems with complex behaviors, such as a vending machine. State diagrams can represent the different states the machine can be in, transitions between states, and the events that trigger those transitions.

12.6.2 State Diagrams:

Question 3: How do interaction diagrams, such as collaboration and sequence diagrams, differ in their representation and use?
Answer 3: Collaboration diagrams focus on visualizing the structural organization of objects and their interactions, emphasizing the structure of the system. Sequence diagrams, on the other hand, depict the chronological order of messages exchanged between objects, emphasizing dynamic behavior. The choice between them depends on the modeling focus.

Question 4: In what scenarios would you choose to use interaction diagrams, and how do they support the modeling of complex system behavior?
Answer 4: Interaction diagrams are beneficial when you need to model complex interactions and dependencies between objects or components in a system. They provide a clear and chronological representation of how objects communicate, making them valuable for understanding and designing systems with intricate behavior.

Question 5: How does UML's advanced structured modeling contribute to the design, analysis, and documentation phases of a software project?
Answer 5: Advanced structured modeling in UML contributes by offering a deeper understanding of the system's behavior, aiding in design validation and error detection. It supports effective documentation by providing visual representations of complex behavior, which can be used for reference and communication throughout the project's lifecycle.

12.7 Use Case Diagrams

12.7.1 Use Cases and Actors:

Question 1: What is a use case, and how is it represented in a UML use case diagram?
Answer 1: A use case is a description of a specific interaction between a user or actor and a system. In a UML use case diagram, a use case is represented as an oval shape with a name inside, depicting a distinct functionality or scenario of the system.

Question 2: Can you explain the role of actors in use case diagrams, and provide an example of actors in a real-world scenario?
Answer 2: Actors in use case diagrams represent external entities (users, systems, or devices) interacting with the system. For example, in an online shopping system, the "Customer" and "Administrator" are actors as they interact with the system to perform actions like making purchases or managing products.

12.7.2 Use Case Relationships:

Question 3: What are the primary relationships used in UML use case diagrams, and how do they connect use cases and actors?
Answer 3: UML use case diagrams employ relationships such as "association," "include," and "extend." "Association" shows the communication between actors and use cases, while "include" and "extend" describe the interactions between use cases themselves, with "include" indicating mandatory interactions and "extend" showing optional extensions.

Question 4: How do "include" and "extend" relationships differ in use case diagrams, and when would you choose one over the other?
Answer 4: In a use case diagram, "include" relationships are used when one use case must always include another use case to achieve its functionality. "Extend" relationships, on the other hand, describe optional extensions that may or may not occur, depending on specific conditions or scenarios.

Question 5: What is the significance of the "generalization" relationship in use case diagrams, and how does it affect the modeling of use cases?
Answer 5: The "generalization" relationship is used to show that one use case is a specialized version of another use case, inheriting its properties and behaviors. It helps in reusing and organizing use cases, making the diagram more concise and manageable.

Question 6: Can you describe a real-world example where use case diagrams were used to model and document system interactions effectively?
Answer 6: In an airline reservation system, use case diagrams can represent interactions between actors like "Passenger," "Reservation Clerk," and "System Administrator" and use cases like "Make Reservation," "Cancel Reservation," and "Manage User Accounts." This visual representation clarifies how the system functions and how various users interact with it.

Question 7: How do use case diagrams aid in system requirements analysis and validation?
Answer 7: Use case diagrams help in identifying and validating system requirements by providing a clear visual representation of how users or actors interact with the system. They enable stakeholders to review and refine the requirements, ensuring that the system aligns with their needs.

Question 8: How can use case diagrams be utilized in the early stages of software development, such as during requirements gathering and analysis?
Answer 8: Use case diagrams are valuable during requirements gathering and analysis as they provide a visual context for discussing and documenting system functionalities. They help in clarifying user needs and serve as a foundation for designing the system's structure.

Question 9: What are some best practices for creating effective use case diagrams that are easy to understand and maintain?
Answer 9: Best practices include keeping use cases concise, using clear and descriptive names, organizing use cases logically, and avoiding excessive detail in the diagram. Additionally, involving stakeholders in the use case development process ensures that the diagram accurately reflects user interactions.

Question 10: How does the use case diagram relate to other UML diagrams, and how can they be integrated to provide a comprehensive view of a software system?
Answer 10: The use case diagram is often the starting point for modeling a system, providing an overview of user interactions. It can be complemented by other UML diagrams, such as class diagrams, sequence diagrams, and activity diagrams, which provide in-depth insights into the system's structure and behavior. Integrating these diagrams offers a holistic view of the software system.

12.8 Object-Oriented Concepts and Principles

Question 1: What are the core principles of object-oriented programming, and how do they contribute to software design?
Answer 1: The core principles of object-oriented programming (OOP) are encapsulation, inheritance, and polymorphism. These principles promote modularity, code reusability, and the modeling of real-world objects in software design.

Question 2: Can you explain the concept of encapsulation in OOP and its importance in software development?
Answer 2: Encapsulation is the principle of bundling data and methods that operate on that data into a single unit, known as a class. It restricts direct access to an object's internal details, promoting data integrity, and code maintenance.

Question 3: How does inheritance in OOP facilitate code reuse and the creation of class hierarchies?
Answer 3: Inheritance allows a class to inherit the properties and behaviors of another class. This promotes code reuse and enables the creation of class hierarchies, where a superclass (base class) defines common attributes and methods shared by its subclasses (derived classes).

Question 4: What is polymorphism in OOP, and how does it enhance the flexibility and extensibility of software systems?
Answer 4: Polymorphism allows objects of different classes to be treated as instances of a common superclass. It enhances flexibility by enabling the same method to have different implementations in different classes. This promotes extensibility and adaptability in software systems.

Question 5: How does the concept of abstraction simplify complex systems and aid in software modeling?
Answer 5: Abstraction is the process of simplifying complex systems by focusing on the essential properties and behaviors while ignoring irrelevant details. It aids in software modeling by providing a high-level view of a system's structure and behavior.

Question 6: What is the significance of the "is-a" relationship in object-oriented design, and how is it realized through inheritance?
Answer 6: The "is-a" relationship represents the concept of generalization in object-oriented design, where a subclass "is-a" specific type of the superclass. Inheritance is the mechanism that realizes this relationship, allowing subclasses to inherit properties and behaviors from their super classes.

Question 7: How do object-oriented principles align with real-world modeling and make it easier to represent complex systems?
Answer 7: Object-oriented principles, such as encapsulation, inheritance, and polymorphism, align with real-world modeling by allowing software to mimic real-world objects and their interactions. This modeling approach simplifies system representation and makes it more intuitive.

Question 8: Can you provide an example of a real-world scenario where object-oriented concepts and principles were applied effectively in software development?
Answer 8: In a video game development project, object-oriented principles can be used to model game objects like "Player," "Enemy," and "Power-Up." Encapsulation ensures that the internal state of each object is protected, inheritance helps create specialized characters, and polymorphism allows interactions like movement and combat to be adapted based on the object type.

Question 9: How do object-oriented design patterns relate to the principles of OOP, and how can they assist in solving common software design problems?
Answer 9: Object-oriented design patterns are recurring solutions to common design problems. They align with OOP principles by promoting modularity, extensibility, and reusability. Design patterns provide proven templates for addressing various software design challenges.

Question 10: How can understanding object-oriented concepts and principles lead to more maintainable and scalable software systems?
Answer 10: Understanding object-oriented concepts and principles allows developers to create well-structured, modular code that is easier to maintain and extend. By modeling software based on real-world objects and using principles like encapsulation and inheritance, systems become more adaptable and scalable over time.

12.9 Object-Oriented Projects Metrics and Estimation

Question 1: What are software metrics in the context of object-oriented development, and how do they help in managing and evaluating project progress?
Answer 1: Software metrics in object-oriented development are quantitative measures that assess various aspects of software quality, such as code complexity, maintainability, and performance. They assist in project management by providing objective data for evaluating the project's progress and quality.

Question 2: Can you explain the significance of software size metrics, such as lines of code (LOC) and function points (FP), in object-oriented projects?
Answer 2: Software size metrics quantify the scale and complexity of a software project. LOC measures the length of code, while FP measures the functionality delivered. These metrics aid in estimating project effort, tracking progress, and comparing projects of similar size and functionality.

Question 3: What are estimation techniques commonly used in object-oriented project management, and how do they contribute to project planning and resource allocation?
Answer 3: Estimation techniques like Function Point Analysis (FPA) and Use Case Points (UCP) are often used in object-oriented projects. They help in project planning by estimating project size, effort, and resource requirements, allowing for better resource allocation and schedule management.

Question 4: How does the concept of "velocity" in agile development relate to project estimation in object-oriented development, and what benefits does it offer?
Answer 4: Velocity in agile development is a measure of a team's capacity to complete work in a specific time frame. It's relevant to project estimation in object-oriented development as it provides data on how much work can be accomplished in an iteration. This data aids in accurate estimation and improved planning, especially in agile methodologies.

Question 5: Can you describe a real-world example where object-oriented project metrics and estimation techniques were applied to improve project management and deliver a successful software system?
Answer 5: In the development of an e-commerce platform, object-oriented project metrics were used to estimate the size and complexity of the system. The team used function points and historical data to estimate project effort accurately. This improved resource allocation, schedule adherence, and ultimately led to the successful delivery of the system within the expected timeframe.

Online Resources

Chapter 12 YouTube Playlist Link:
Link: https://www.youtube.com/playlist?list=PLzlh_31VWEFpcvF7V40zYcZCHQbvZR11h
QR Code:

Online Exam Paper Link:
Link: https://forms.gle/oDghydFGBn8oBQKK7
QR Code:

MCQ Video Playlist Link:
Link: https://youtu.be/t0dI72aFIAQ
QR Code:

True/False Video Playlist Link:
Link: https://youtu.be/LmuCwTjjQT0
QR Code:

Online MCQ Exam Paper Link:
Link: https://forms.office.com/r/85JJCMS7Mc
QR Code:

Online True/False Exam Paper Link:
Link: **https://forms.office.com/r/8vrDKNMzbt**
QR Code:

Additional Resources

YouTube Videos Playlists for all Chapters:

Chapter 1 Video Playlist Link:
Link: https://www.youtube.com/playlist?list=PLzlh_31VWEFoI3TvpCR1YV5zPoqIlSV_e
QR Code:

Chapter 2 Video Playlist Link:
Link: https://www.youtube.com/playlist?list=PLzlh_31VWEFpO9Cc5Av_iP4FUcMcYXlWG
QR Code:

Chapter 3 Video Playlist Link:
Link: https://www.youtube.com/playlist?list=PLzlh_31VWEFrArOJ-tZRk9Ex3SOWzFog1
QR Code:

Chapter 4 Video Playlist Link:
Link: https://www.youtube.com/playlist?list=PLzlh_31VWEFps2eNLdR36zxZZ2UnXiMb3
QR Code:

Chapter 5 Video Playlist Link:
Link: https://www.youtube.com/playlist?list=PLzlh_31VWEFqcHMJdHsQm1NxsE0ugxVik
QR Code:

Chapter 6 Video Playlist Link:
Link: https://www.youtube.com/playlist?list=PLzlh_31VWEFoE6zOQD-kGLWJZ65MuTrZz
QR Code:

Chapter 7 Video Playlist Link:
Link: https://www.youtube.com/playlist?list=PLzlh_31VWEFrAS1b7aFQ0Dr9K0uIH1tLY
QR Code:

Chapter 8 Video Playlist Link:
Link: https://www.youtube.com/playlist?list=PLzlh_31VWEFo_-YP3k45xd9fLCxZuO6zf
QR Code:

Chapter 9 Video Playlist Link:
Link: https://www.youtube.com/playlist?list=PLzlh_31VWEFrHzSFXM2p559CFr2Bxk8WC
QR Code:

Chapter 10 Video Playlist Link:
Link: https://www.youtube.com/playlist?list=PLzlh_31VWEFoFGTiNRypX3swnvzQCEqdY
QR Code:

Chapter 11 Video Playlist Link:
Link: https://www.youtube.com/playlist?list=PLzlh_31VWEFp-MPUQG8kjY2CcpclIMc7q
QR Code:

Chapter 12 Video Playlist Link:
Link: https://www.youtube.com/playlist?list=PLzlh_31VWEFpcvF7V40zYcZCHQbvZR11h
QR Code:

Playlist of all Chapters MCQ's and True/False Practice Questions:
Link: https://studio.youtube.com/playlist/PLzlh_31VWEFoAD-X1HXoHJN80R1mDgC1G/videos
QR Code:

Software Engineering Interview Videos Playlist-
Link: https://www.youtube.com/playlist?list=PLzlh_31VWEFpMoUmeqchKtcSL4QXE8RWM
QR Code:

© Author and Publisher 2024